iPhone 11, 11 Pro & 11 Pro Max For The Elderly

A Comprehensive Illustrated, Practical Guide with Tips & Tricks to Mastering The iPhone 11 Series And iOS 13

Michael Hill

Contents

A Brief Review of iPhone 11, 11 Pro & 11 Pro Max

The iPhone 11 series is the largest and most powerful phone Apple's ever created, taking the very best of its technology and combining it with an upgraded design that includes a new matte back, three cameras designed to rival the best from Google and Huawei, 4K video at 60 frames per second with extended dynamic range, Better sound from the phone's speakers and an enhanced battery for greater endurance.

iPhone 11

With the added ultra-wide camera and Night Mode, improved selfies, industry-leading A13 Bionic chipset, Gigabit LTE and Wi-Fi 6, and iOS 13 operating system, all starting at $699, iPhone 11 is the most compelling iPhone Apple has ever made.

It's so close in capabilities to the iPhone 11 Pro that only display, camera, and radio nerds may really notice any day-to-day differences. For this review, I want to focus on what makes the iPhone 11 the new iPhone for everyone. Everyone who has an iPhone 6 or earlier and is looking for a new phone to keep getting the latest updates. Who has an iPhone 6s or iPhone 7, and is thinking it's time to trade in and move up.

Who might even have an iPhone 8 and is finally ready to give up the Home button, or an iPhone X, and wants a dual-camera system that's just a little brighter and wider, or maybe even a return to LCD.

Ultimately, it's about figuring out what's right for you, or for you and your family. And that's what this brief review is here to help answer.

At a glance, the iPhone 11 looks almost identical to last year's iPhone XR in size and shape. It's got a bigger, better camera — two of them again — and a bigger, matte camera bump to go with them.

The Home button, forehead, and chin, are still gone, as is the headphone jack. But, these days that's the norm, not the exception.

It's still Lightning, not USB-C, and still includes a 5 watt USB-A charger, not the beefier 18 watt USB-PD charger now included with the Pro. Though, if you pick one up separately, you can fast-charge to 50% in just 30 minutes. You can also still charge inductively with a Qi pad at the same 7.5 watts as last year.

The speakers are new and offer spatial audio, which will precisely place 5.1 surround or Dolby Atmos sound to precisely match any video that supports it.

The notch is still here, but now it houses an even faster, more reliable Face ID and a wider, 12MP selfie cam that goes to up to 4K and, yeah, shoots slow-mo selfie video.

Glossy, glassy black and white are still options, but there's also a paler yellow this year, and a slightly different Product Red. Sky blue and coral orange are gone, though, replaced with a lavender purple and mint green.

That glass is also tougher, so hopefully harder to scratch or shatter. Water resistance is still 30 minutes but up from IP67 and one meter to IP68 and two meters. Just take it easy dropping it in the deep end.

Apple says the battery will last an hour longer than the iPhone XR, which — ugh, math — makes it 2.5 hours longer than the iPhone 8 Plus. Roughly 17 hours of local video, 10 hours of streaming video, and 65 hours of wireless audio. Thanks to the huge leaps forward in the Pro models, the 6.1-inch iPhone is no longer the battery life leader, but it packs plenty of power.

There's still a dual SIM, one nanoSIM card, one eSIM. I know some people want dual cards. I can't wait for dual e, but it's upgraded to Gigabit LTE, up to 38% faster Wi-Fi 6, and up to 45% longer-range beam-forming Bluetooth.

It's also packing Apple's top-of-the-line, industry leading chipset, the A13 Bionic. A13's efficiency, performance, graphics, and neural cores aren't just 20% faster each, they use 40, 25, 30, and 15% less power respectively. It also has 4GB of memory instead of 3GB like on the XR, and brings with it a machine-learned ton of new photographic and other features we'll get to in just a few minutes.

Storage options remain the same at 64, 128, and 256 GB, but the price is now

$50 cheaper for all of them. So, go for at least 128. You'll thank me later.

I've been using a purple iPhone 11 review unit running iOS 13.0 for almost a week, both while traveling in California and here at home in Montreal, Canada.

And there's a lot here to credit here, but also a good amount still to critique.

The iPhone 11 is For people who want:

- Edge-to-edge design with gesture navigation.
- Dual-camera system with wide and ultra-wide angles
- Depth-aware front-facing camera.
- Face ID biometrics.
- A 6.1-inch display.
- Industry-leading performance

- Colors!

Not for people who want:

- Classic iPhone design with Home button.
- Triple-camera system with telephoto angle.
- No notch.
- Fingerprint identity biometrics.
- An OLED display.
- Android

iPhone 11 Pro & 11 Pro Max

Once upon a time, the iPhone was the best camera you had with you. Now, Apple flat out wants to make it the best camera, period. What they can't do physically with enormous lenses and sensors, they're doing computationally with ridiculously optimized silicon and machine learning. And not just by taking the iPhone to 11, but by making it pro: The iPhone 11 Pro.

Everything that's already packed into the 6.1-inch iPhone 11 is here as well, but escalated significantly: 5.8- and 6.5-inch higher-density, higher contrast, higher brightness, and extreme dynamic range OLED displays; a triple imaging system with ultra wide-angle, wide-angle, and telephoto cameras; 4x4 MIMO LTE; a full 4 meters of water resistance; up to 512 GB of storage; textured finishes that look more like metal than glass; and battery life that's boosted by a jaw-dropping 4 and 5 hours respectively.

Those differences may not mean much to most people and that's fine. I'd argue that's even the point. Today, you can get a top-shelf iPhone 11 for $699, and in a wider variety of colors too.

But, if you're the type of person who wants the best of the best, the ultimate expression of the iPhone technology and experience today, you can reach for the absolute rafters with the $999 iPhone 11 Pro or $1099 iPhone 11 Pro Max.

In addition to everything I included in my preamble to the iPhone 11 review, here's what you need to know about the Pros. Right off the bat, the iPhone 11 Pro and iPhone 11 Pro Max look just about identical to last year's iPhone XS and iPhone XS Max. Same sizes, same shapes. They've just got three cameras on the back now instead of two, and a giant, glossy back camera bump to go with them.

The port is still Lightning, but the cable in the box now ends with USB-C and comes with a new, 18-watt adapter that fast-charges to 50% in just 30 min.

The glass backs are textured now, and matte, which looks almost like the aluminum finishes of old. And, while there are still silver, space gray, and gold options, there's also a brand new midnight green.

Ingress protection is still IP68 and certified for up to 30 minutes, but for up to 4 meters of water now, not just two. Fear no deep end of the pool.

Apple says the batteries on the iPhone 11 Pro and iPhone 11 Pro Max will last —

wait for it — 4 and 5 hours longer than last year's iPhone XS and XS Max. And no, that's not a typo. I checked. Thrice: Up to 18 hours of local video playback for the Pro and 20 for the Max, 11 hours and 12 hours of video streaming, and 65 and 80 hours of wireless audio. All hail the new battery champions.

The already 4x4 MIMO — multi in, multi-out — LTE now runs up to 1.6 Gbps, so you can really get your carrier aggregation on.

Storage options are the same at 64, 256, and 512 GB, as are the price points, starting at $999 and $1099.

I've been using an iPhone 11 Pro and iPhone 11 Pro in midnight green, running iOS 13.0, since the Apple Event last week

— and yes, with my own personal SIM cards in all of the phones, all the time, traveling from California and home here in Montreal.

And while there's a ton I absolutely love about them, there's also a ton I'd really like to love more. Or, maybe, just want more to love?

The iPhone 11 Pro and Pro Max is For people who want:

- Extreme Dynamic Range OLED display.
- 6.5-inch display option.
- Triple-camera system with telephoto.
- Depth-aware front-facing camera.
- Face ID biometrics.
- Midnight Green!

Not for people who want:

- Home button.

- 90 or 120Hz display.

- Fingerprint identity biometrics.

- Low, low pricing.

- USB-C

- Android

That is our brief review. This comprehensive Manual is essentially to help you with tips and tricks to maximize your device.

Getting Started

Whether you're brand new to the Apple ecosystem or upgrading for the tenth time, setting up a new iPhone is an exhilarating experience, not unlike waking up on Christmas morning. From the moment you see that first "Hello" to the final step, here's everything you need to know about setting up your new iPhone 11, 11 Pro & 11 Pro Max.

How To Set Up Your New iPhone 11, 11 Pro & 11 Pro Max

You can set up your new iPhone 11 in one of three ways, start fresh, restore from another iPhone, or import content from a non-Apple phone. Here's what each of those options mean in more detail.

- **Set up as new** - means starting everything — every setting — from scratch. This is for people who've never used a smartphone or online services before or who want their iPhone to feel truly brand new.

- **Restore from a previous iPhone, iPad, or iPod touch backup** - You can do this online with iCloud or over USB with iTunes. This is for people who've had a previous iOS device and are moving to a new one.

- **Import from Android, BlackBerry, or Windows Phone** - Apple has an app in Google Play to make Android easier, but online services let you move a lot of data over from any old device. This is for people switching to iPhone or iPad.

The moment you turn on your new iPhone for the first time, you'll be greeted with "Hello" in a variety of languages. It's the same whether you're starting from scratch, restoring from another iPhone, or switching from Android.

- Touch **slide to set up** and slide your finger across the screen to get started.
- Select your **language**.
- Select your **country or region**.
- Select a **wi-fi network**. If you are not in a wi-fi network range, you can set this up later. Select **Cellular** instead. However, here is how to set up Wi-Fi:
  - Tap **Settings** > **Wi-Fi**
  - Tap the **network name** you want to join
  - Type the password and tap **Join**. If you don't know the password, it might be on a sticker on the router.

- A tick shows when you are connected

- At this point, you can choose to use automatic set up to set up your new iPhone with the same passcode and settings as another iPhone. If you choose to set up your new iPhone manually, continue with the following steps.

- Tap **Continue** after reading about Apple's Data & Privacy information.

- Tap **Enable Location Services**. If you don't want to enable location services at this time, select **Skip Location Services**. You can enable certain location services manually, like Maps.

- Set up **Face ID**. If you need help, here's how to set up Face ID on your new iPhone XS, iPhone XS Max, or iPhone XR.
  - Tap **Get Started** and hold the phone so your face is in the camera frame
  - Move your head slowly around to fill the circle of green bars, then tap **continue**.
  - Scab your face again, moving it around to fill the green bars again.
  - When Face ID is set up, tap **Continue**.
- Create a **Passcode**. You can set up a standard six-digit passcode, or create a four-digit passcode or custom passcode by tapping **Passcode Options**.

You'll next be asked if you want to restore from a backup, set up as a new iPhone, or move data from Android.

Restoring Or Transfering Your Data From Another Phone

If you're not going to start fresh with a brand new data-clean device, you're going to want to transfer your data from your old iPhone to your new one, or transfer data from your old Android device to your new iPhone. Here's how.

How to restore Data from an iCloud or iTunes Backup

It's time to decide how you want to transfer your old iPhone's data. You have two choices when restoring your apps and data from another iPhone; iCloud or iTunes.

Which one you choose depends on whether you backup your old iPhone in iCloud or by plugging it into your computer and backing it up via iTunes.

The key here is to make sure your old iPhone has been backed up first. After you've backed up your old iPhone, select whether you want to restore your new iPhone from iCloud or iTunes.

Transfering Your Data To Your New iPhone Using iCloud

If you use Apple's online service, iCloud, to back up your iPhone, then you can transfer all your data over wirelessly. Depending on when your last backup was, however, you might want to manually trigger a backup before making a transfer.

That'll ensure everything is as up-to-date as possible.

- Open **Settings** on your **old** iPhone.
- Tap the **Apple ID banner**.
- Tap **iCloud**.

- Tap **iCloud Backup**.
- Tap **Back Up Now**.

- Turn your **old iPhone** off once the backup is finished.
- Remove the **SIM card** from your old iPhone or if you're going to move it to your new one

Wait for the backup to complete before proceeding.

You can now set aside your old iPhone. Make sure that your new iPhone is off when you start these next steps.

- Insert your old **SIM card** into your new iPhone if you want to move it between devices.

- Turn on your **new iPhone**.

- Slide up or press the **Home button** depending on which device you're setting up.

- Follow the directions to choose your language and set up your Wi-Fi network.

- Tap **Restore from iCloud backup**.

- Sign in to your **iCloud account** (This is your Apple ID).

- Tap **Next**.

- Tap **Agree**.

- Tap **Agree** again.

- Choose the **backup** you just made.

Depending on how much data you have to re-download, including music and apps, it might take a while for the transfer to complete. Stay on Wi-Fi as much as possible to speed up the process.

Your iPhone might feel warm for a while, and battery life may take a big initial hit. Don't worry, that's the radios and processors working overtime to get everything back in place, and the Spotlight search system indexing it as fast as it can.

Transfering Your Data to Your New iPhone Using iTunes

Here's the deal: If you make an encrypted backup of your old iPhone using iTunes, then restore it to your new iPhone, it'll bring most — if not all — your password information along with it. That'll save you a lot of time and effort getting set back up.

You do need a Lightning to USB cable (or 30-pin Dock to USB if you have an iPhone 4s or earlier), and you'll still have to re-download apps — the App Store gives you slightly different versions for each device, optimized to run best on that specific hardware — but overall I still find it to be much, much faster.

- Make sure you're running the most recent version of iTunes.
- Plug your **old iPhone** into your Mac or Windows PC.
- Launch **iTunes**.
- Click on the **iPhone icon** in the menu bar when it appears.
- Click on **Encrypt Backup**; you'll be asked to add a password if this is your first time encrypting a backup.
- Click on **Back Up Now**.
- Skip **Backup Apps**, if asked. (They'll likely re-download anyway.)
- Unplug your **old iPhone** when done.
- Turn off your **old iPhone**.
- Take your **SIM card** out of your **old iPhone**. (If you don't have a new or

separate SIM card for your new phone.)

- Wait for the backup to complete before proceeding.
- Put your **SIM card** into your **new iPhone**. (If it didn't come with a new or different SIM card.)
- Turn on your **new iPhone**.
- Plug your **new iPhone** into your Mac or Windows PC.
- **Slide to set up** on your **iPhone**.
- Follow the directions to choose your language and set up your Wi-Fi network.
- Select **Restore from iTunes backup**.

- On **iTunes** on your Mac or Windows PC, select **Restore from this backup**.
- Choose your **recent backup** from the list.
- Click **Continue**.
- Enter your **password** if your backup was encrypted and it asks.

Keep your iPhone plugged into iTunes until the transfer is complete, and on Wi-Fi until all re-downloads are complete. Depending on how much data you have to re-download, including music and apps, it might take a while.

Your iPhone might feel warm or even hot, and you might burn a lot of battery life for the first few hours or even a day or due to the radios working and the

Spotlight search system indexing. Just let it finish.

How To Move Data From An Android Device To iPhone Or iPad With Move To iOS

If you're switching from an Android-based operating system, first let me welcome you to the Apple family.

Apple has a special app just for people switching from Android called Move to iOS and it's available in the Google Play store. Before moving your data to your new iPhone, download Move to iOS on your Android phone.

Moving your photos, contacts, calendars, and accounts from your old Android phone or tablet to your new iPhone or iPad is easier than ever with Apple's Move to iOS app. Apple's first Android app, it hooks your old Android and new Apple device together over a direct Wi-Fi connection and transfers over all your data. The following steps will guide you:

1. Set up your iPhone or iPad until you reach the screen titled "Apps & Data".

2. Tap "Move Data from Android" option.

3. On your **Android phone or tablet**, open the **Google Play Store** and search for **Move to iOS**.

4. Open the **Move to iOS app listing**.

5. Tap **Install**

6. Tap to accept the permissions request.

7. Tap **Open** after it's installed.

8. Tap **Continue** on both devices.

9. Tap **Agree** and then **Next** on the Android phone or tablet.

10. On your **Android device**, enter the **12-digit code** displayed on the **iPhone or iPad**.

After entering the code, the Android device will connect with your iPhone or iPad over a peer-to-peer Wi-Fi connection and determine what data will be transferred.

It will ask whether you want to transfer your Google Account info (so that you can quickly log in on your new Apple device), Chrome bookmarks, text messages, contacts, and the photos and videos in your camera roll. Select everything you want to move over.

Your Android phone or tablet will transfer the selected data over to your iPhone or iPad and place the appropriate content into the correct apps. The two devices will disconnect and Android will prompt you to take your old device to the Apple Store, where they'll recycle it for free.

Once the transfer process is complete, tap on **Continue Setting Up iPhone** or **Continue Setting Up iPad** on your device and carry on setting up a new Apple ID or logging into your existing one.

Once the setup process is completed, you'll be prompted to log in to the accounts you transferred from your old

Android device. Do that, and then you're good to go!

How long the transfer process takes varies depending on how much data you're transferring — especially if you were storing many photos and videos. I transferred roughly 400MB of files and it took about 8 minutes from starting to set up our iPhone to entering account passwords.

To help you settle in with your new iPhone and iPad, Google has developed several apps that tie into their services, including the full Google Drive and Google Docs suites, Google Play Music, Gmail, and more. Heck, if an **Apple Watch** isn't your thing, you can even bring your old **Android Wear** watch to the iPhone too.

What Happens to The Photos?

Honestly, if you're like me, you may just want to make sure that your photos are transferred from one phone to another. If that's the case, I highly recommend installing Google Photos on your Android phone and syncing all of the photos prior to switching over to the iPhone. Once on the iPhone, merely download Google Photos and download all of those photos to your iPhone.

It's a relatively easy process that ensures you're always going to have your photos, even when disaster strikes, since they're always backed up in the cloud!

What About *Just* The Contacts?

OK, so you don't want to lose those precious contacts you've been hoarding for years and refuse to pare down. I get it — you may still want to contact that ex one day. I don't judge.

If that's the case, and you don't want to go through the hassle of Apple's Move to iOS app, there's always CardDAV, a protocol that Google uses to synchronize its contacts between devices. The iPhone supports this too, so all you'll need is to log into your Google account on the iPhone and follow the instructions.

Get Haptic Feedback When Unlocking Your iPhone with Face ID

Haptic feedback is one of the iPhone's most underrated features. With Face ID, you'll feel a satisfying tap or two when buying something in the App Store or iTunes, unlocking protected notes, viewing saved passwords in Settings, and the list goes on. For the first time, Apple has added haptic feedback when unlocking your iPhone via Face ID, as well as a way to disable haptic feedback entirely.

While there are many instances where haptic feedback from the Taptic Engine is felt using Face ID in iOS 12 and under, that strong vibration when unlocking an iPhone with facial recognition is only on iOS 13, which is still in beta development.

On an iPhone, go to "Accessibility" in the Settings app, then select "Face ID & Attention" under Physical and Motor. A new "Haptic on Successful Activation" toggle will be in those settings. Just enable it, and a satisfying haptic vibration will follow all Face ID authentications.

From what we've discovered, not only will you continue to get tactile haptic feedback for Apple Pay authentication, iTunes and App Store purchases, LastPass authentication, when opening password-protected files in Pages or Numbers, viewing "Website & App Passwords" in Settings, and unlocking secured notes, but you also get that vibratory effect when unlocking your iPhone with your mug.

To disable haptic feedback for Face ID, make sure that toggle above is off. Aside from getting haptic feedback for Face ID device unlocking, this switch in iOS 13 will also kill all haptic feedback when using Face ID. That means all of the examples mentioned above that worked in iOS 12 can be nixed in iOS 13, whereas before there was no way to disable haptic feedback for Apple's facial recognition.

The haptic feedback switch for Face ID is just one of the many new features finding their way to iPhones in iOS 13. Apple has packed over 200 fun changes to the upcoming update, including system-wide dark mode, an overhauled Photos app, and so much more

Turn on Dark Mode

You're going to love the new dark mode in iOS 13. It instantly flips the color scheme, giving you a true back background and white text. Not only is it easy on the eyes, but it also helps with the battery life.

To toggle dark mode, open Control Center, and tap and hold on the Brightness bar. In the bottom-left corner, you'll see a new Appearance toggle. Tap on it to switch to the Dark mode.

Set Custom Schedule for Dark Mode

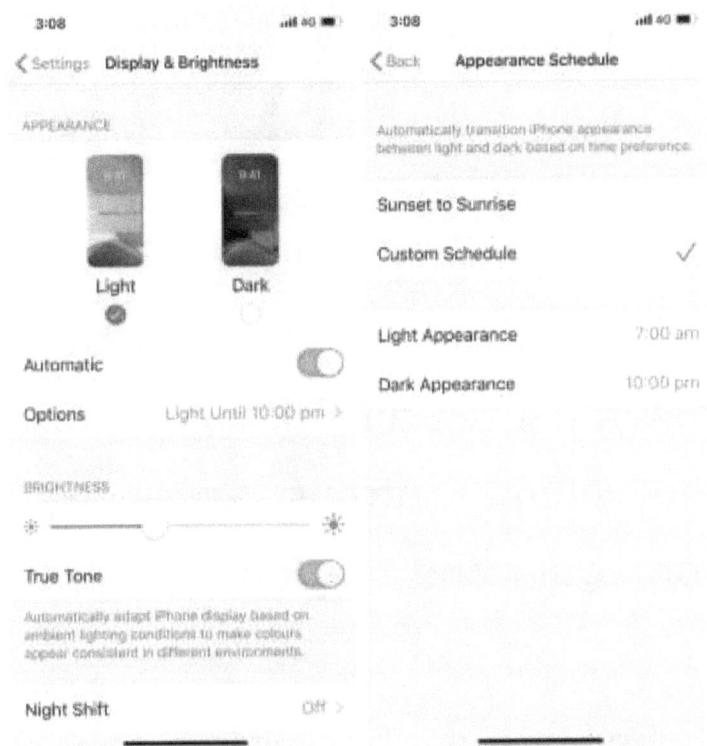

Go to Settings -> Display & Brightness and turn on the Automatic feature. From the new options below, you can set a custom schedule for dark mode based on the sunrise/sunset or a specific time.

Interact With The New Volume HUD

The new Volume HUD gets out of the way. When you first click on the volume button you'll see a thick volume HUD next to the volume buttons. Press the volume button again and the indicator will shrink.

But when it's in the thick stage, you can actually tap and drag on it to quickly change the volume.

Download Files Using Safari

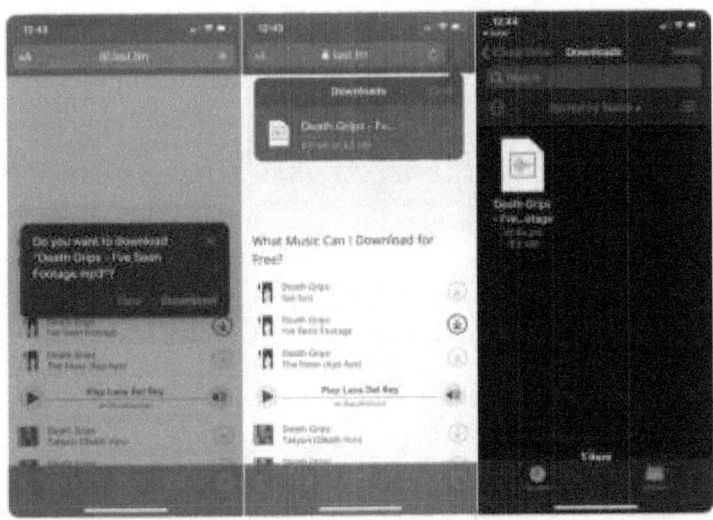

Safari now has a full download manager in iOS 13. When you access a download link, you'll get a popup with a Download button. Tap on it and you'll see a new Downloads section next to the URL bar. You can monitor and control all downloads from here. All downloads are saved to the Downloads folder in iCloud Drive by default.

Change Default File Download Location

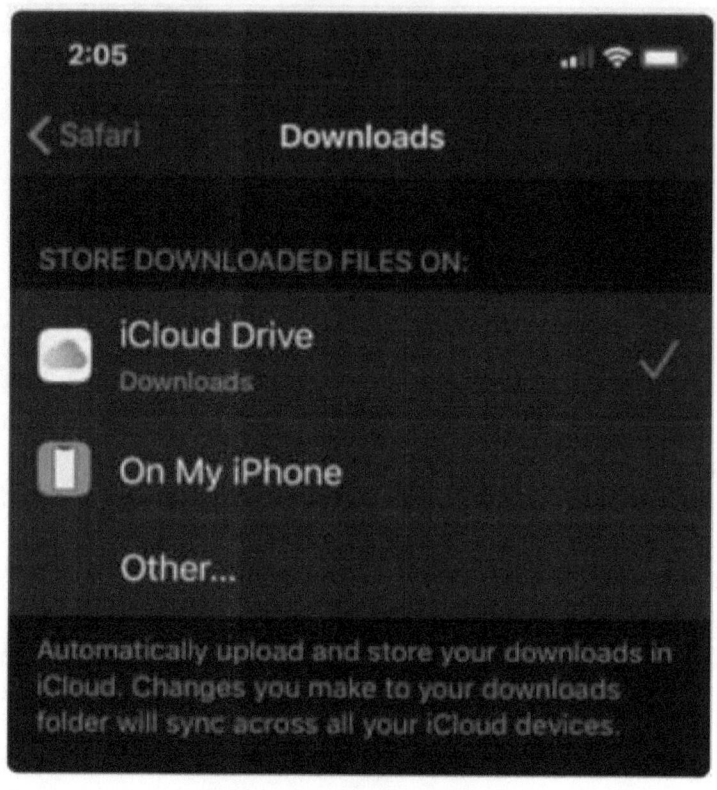

But you can, and should change the default download location in iOS 13. You can even change it to the local storage. Go to Settings -> Safari -> Downloads and switch to On my iPhone. You can also go in and select another folder of your choice.

Use New Cut, Copy, and Paste Gestures

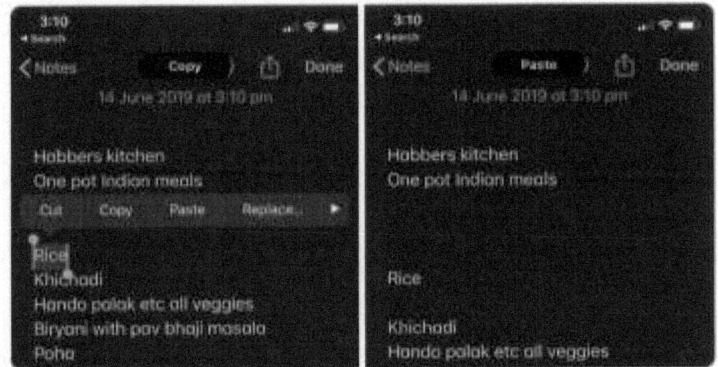

Apple is making text manipulation easier with iOS 13. You can now tap and hold to pick up the cursor and move it around with ease.

Use three finger pinch gesture to copy text, a double three finger pinch gesture to cut text and a three finger expand gesture to paste the text.

Use New Undo and Redo Gestures

Finally, there's a new undo gesture. Just swipe left with three fingers to undo text entry and a three finger right swipe to redo.

Use The New Formatting Bar

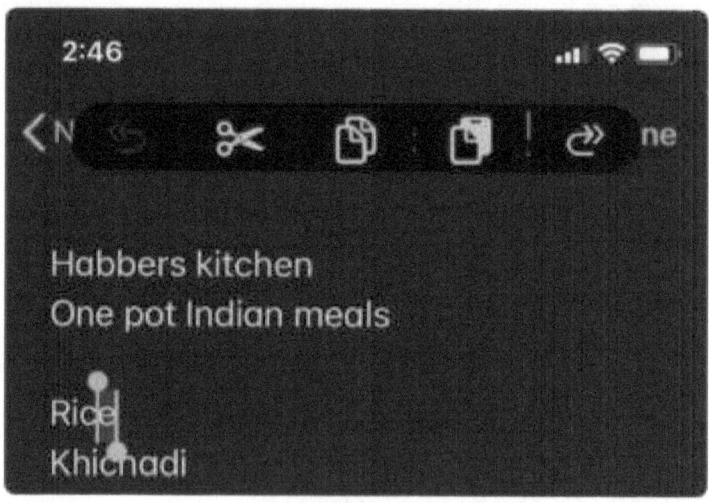

If you don't like swiping, just tap and hold with three fingers to get a new formatting bar. From here, you can easily Cut, Copy, Paste, Undo, and Redo.

The Natural Language Input in New Reminders App

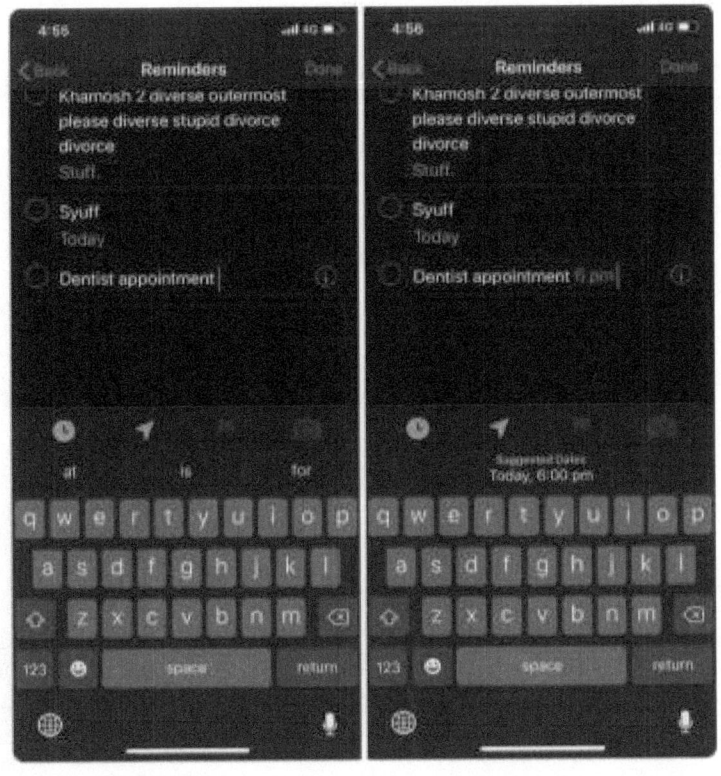

There's a lot to talk about the new Reminders app in iOS 13 but the best new feature is the new text input suggestions. You can type a reminder and then type time and day in the end. You'll see a suggestion in the keyboard field to attach it to the reminders. This is not as great as third party apps but it's better than nothing.

Discover Photos From This Day in Past Years in Photos App

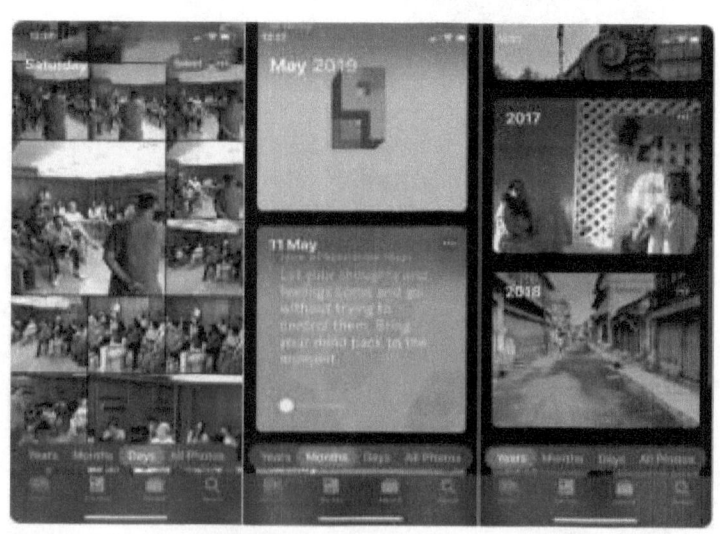

The new Photos app comes with a new All Photos tab, with new sections for Days,

Months and Years. The Years section is the most interesting because it shows one photo from the same day over the past couple of years as a preview.

Replace Snapseed with iOS 13's New Photo Editor

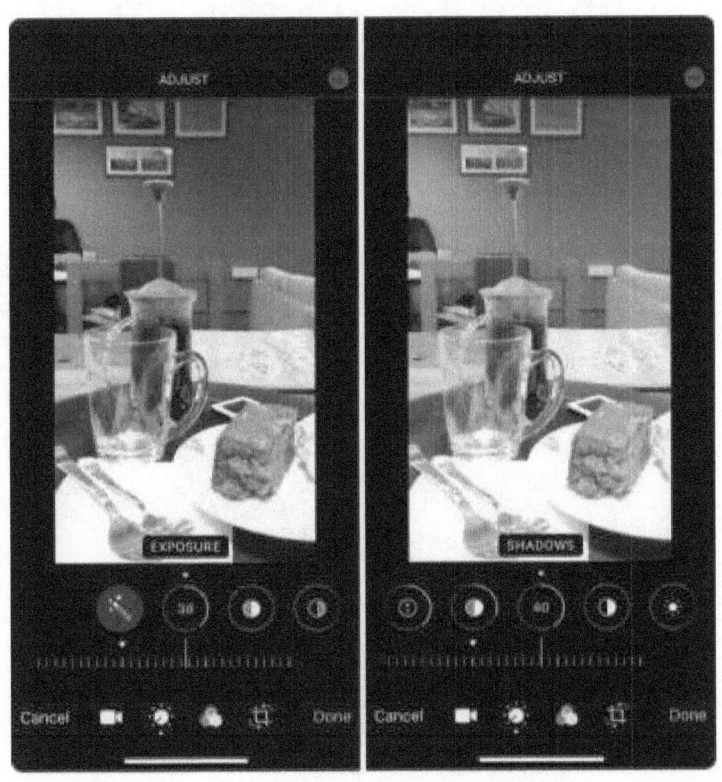

The new Photo editor in iOS 13 is simpler to use and has more editing features. You can now edit the intensity of filters along with elements like brilliance, vibrancy, saturation and more.

If you used an app like Darkroom or Snapseed for basic photo editing (and not the pro level stuff), you can easily replace them with the new photo editor in iOS 13. It's that good.

Edit Videos in the Photos App

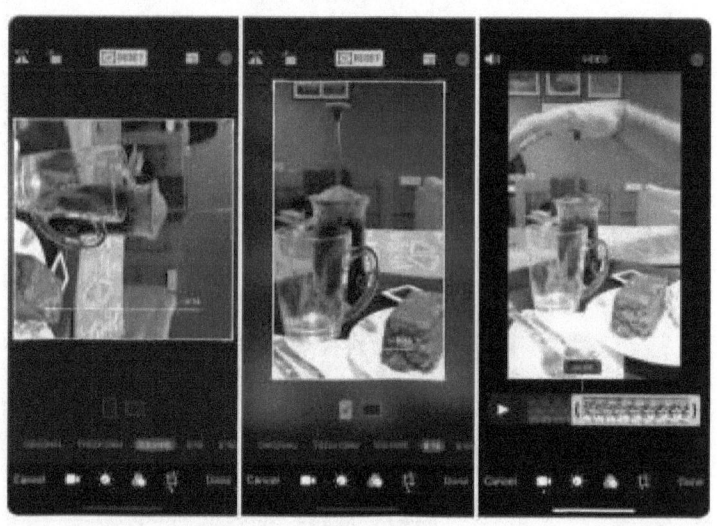

You can also edit videos in the Photos app now. You can easily apply all editing effects from the photo editor, crop the video, set a different aspect ratio, rotate the video and more.

Track Menstrual Cycle in Health App

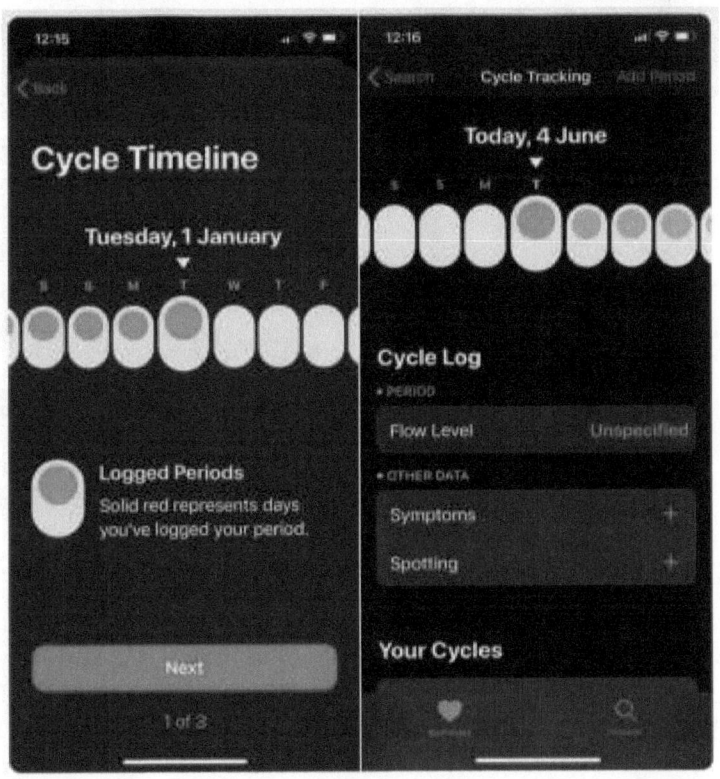

There's a new, fully private menstrual cycle tracking feature in Health app that comes with period tracking, reminders, and fertility tracking as well.

Share Folders from iCloud Drive

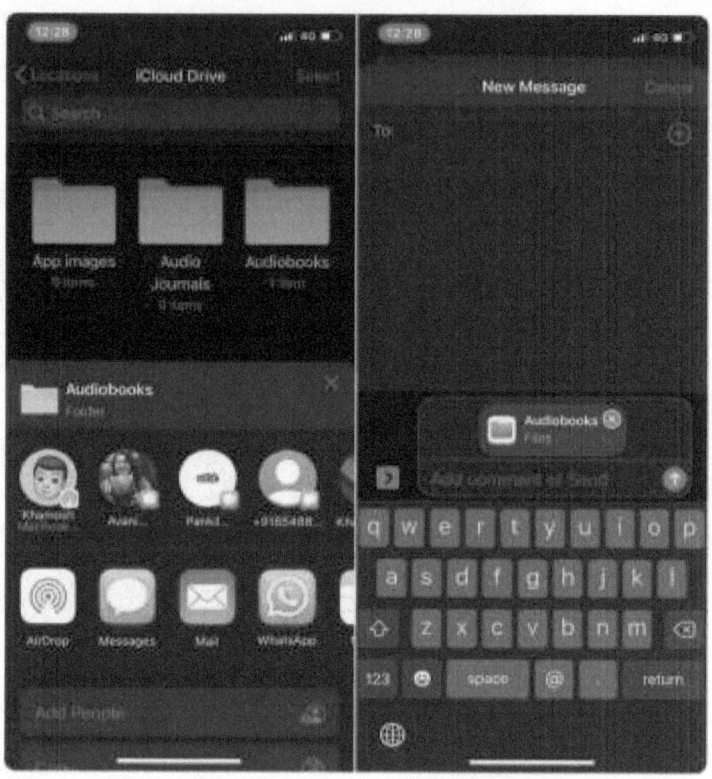

Just like Dropbox, you can now share entire folders with other iCloud Drive users from the Files app. Tap and hold on a folder, select Share -> Add People and choose how you want to invite people to share the folder. Best way to go back is using iMessage or Mail app.

Use Gesture Typing in Keyboard

You can now swipe your finger on the keyboard to type, just like the SwiftKey or Gboard keyboard. This makes one-handed typing much easier.

Disable Bluetooth Access For Apps

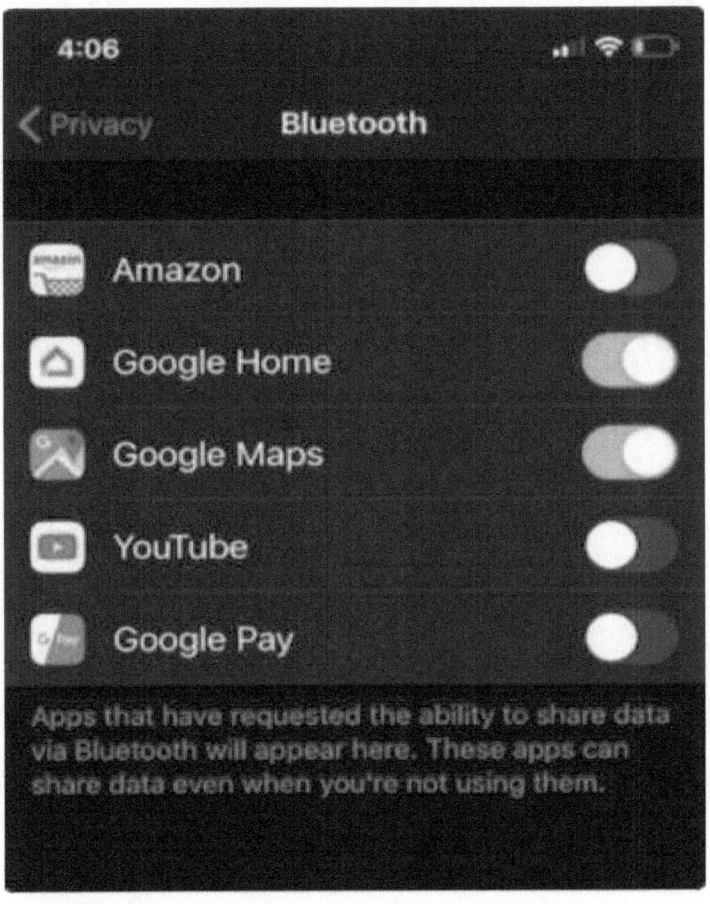

A lot of apps use Bluetooth to figure out and track your location. Not all apps need Bluetooth access, you can now block Bluetooth access for any app when you first launch an app (this has nothing to do with Bluetooth playback). Go to Privacy -> Bluetooth to see all apps that are asking for Bluetooth permissions and you can toggle the access from here as well.

Connect Two AirPods to one iPhone

If you want your friend to listen to the same thing you're playing on your iPhone and you both have AirPods, this process is now much simpler. Just open the AirPlay section from Control Center and flick open the second pair of AirPods to connect and use it alongside your own AirPods.

Set Favorite Locations in Maps

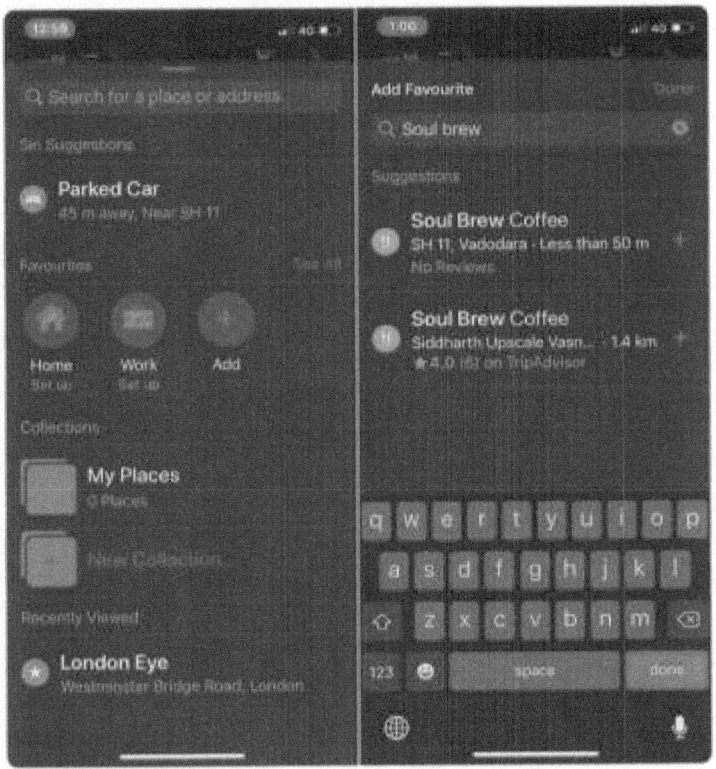

Open the Maps app and you'll see a new Frequent Locations tab. Click on the Add button to search and add a location to this section, to serve as a quick shortcut.

Create Groups of Frequent Places in Maps

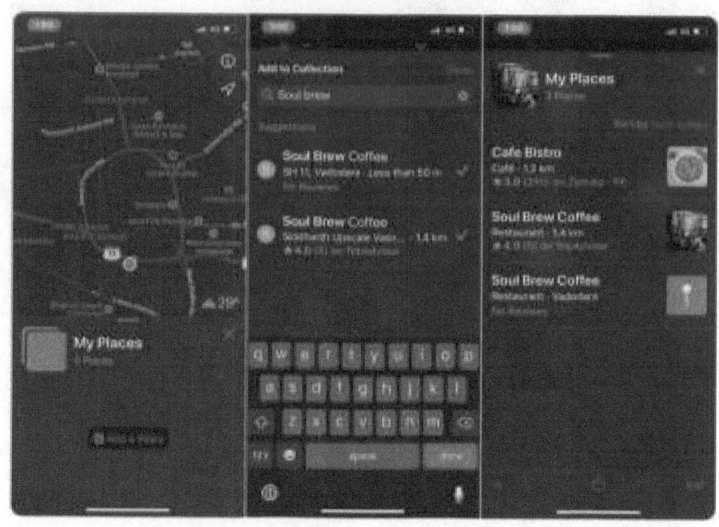

Below, you'll find a new Collections section. You can create a collection and then add places to it. Sharing a collection is easy as well.

Share ETA from Maps App

Just like Google Maps, you can share an ETA with someone using iMessage or Messages. They'll be able to monitor your location from Maps app and will get a message sharing your arrival time.

Track Your Offline Apple Devices Using Find My App

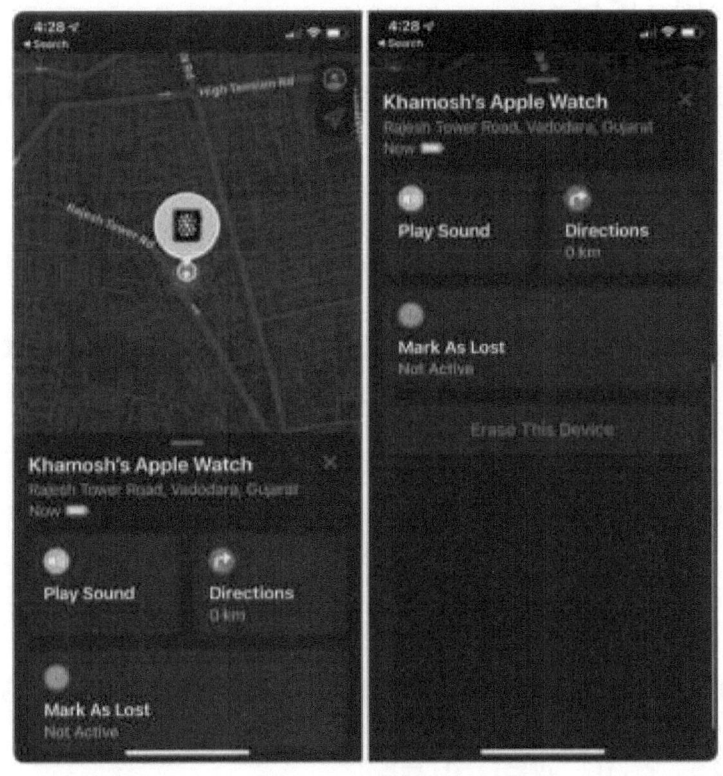

You should know about the new offline device tracking feature in the new Find My app. Just activate the app once and go to settings to make sure the feature is enabled. In the future, you'll be able to track your lost Apple device even if it's offline (using a mesh Bluetooth network). We've talked about the new technology in detail here.

Drag Scrollbar To Quickly Navigate On a Page

The scrollbar in iOS 13 can be picked up and dragged. Tap and move it to quickly jump to any section in the page.

Set Combined App Limits for Screen Time

You can now set an App Limit that is a combination of app categories, specific apps, and websites.

View and Analyze Screen Time Data for Past 30 Days

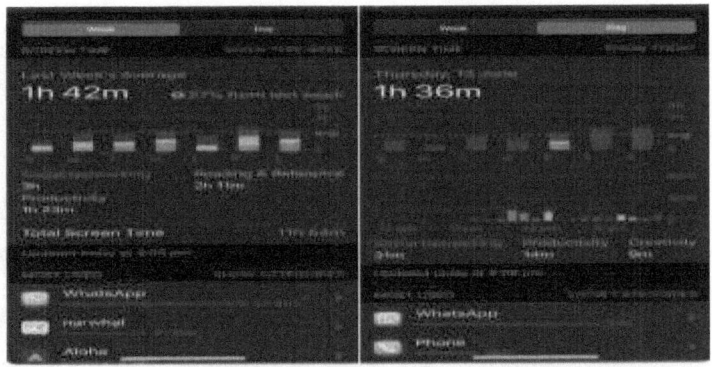

Screen Time data is now available for the past 30 days. This is much better than the old 7 days limit. Open the Screen Time section and you'll be able to switch to the new Week section at the top. Swipe left on the graph to go back in time, week by week, or day by day. As you go back in time, the details below will update as well.

Switch to Open Safari Tab From Search

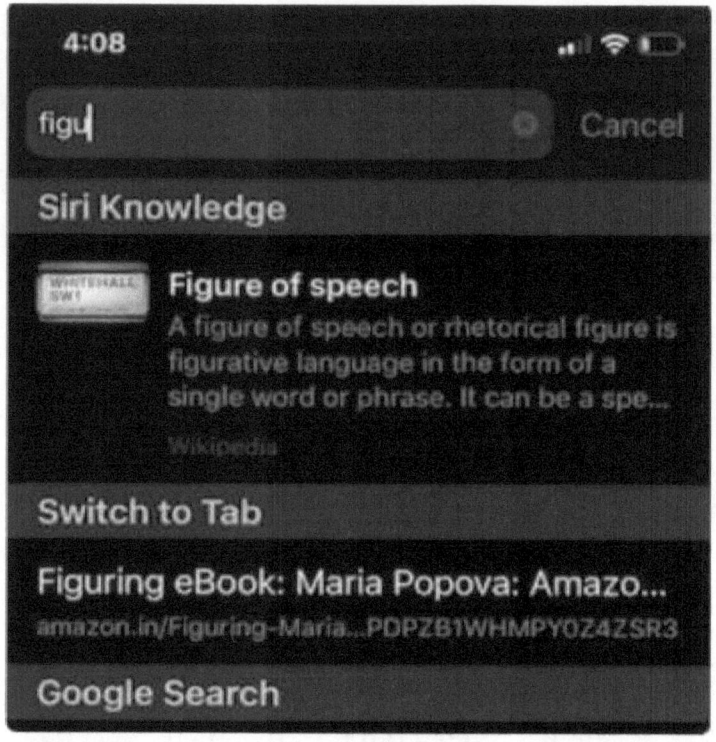

If you can't find a particular tab, just type the tab name in the Smart Search field. Press enter and instead of loading the page again, Safari will take you to the open tab.

Find the Shuffle and Repeat Buttons

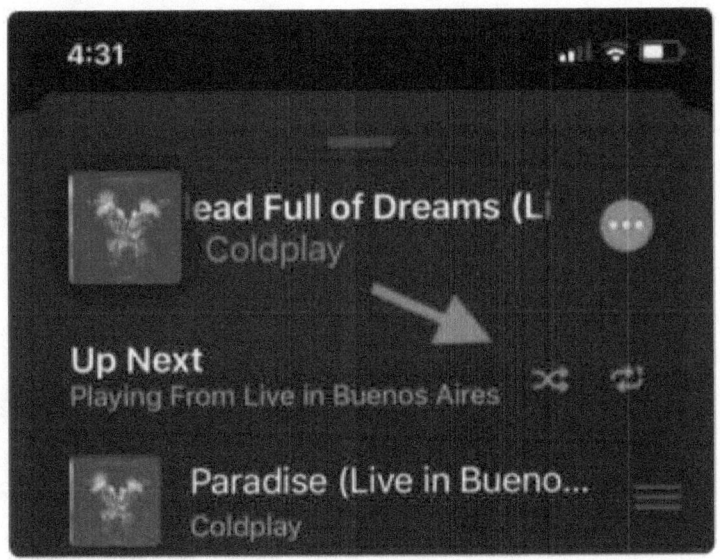

Apple has moved the Shuffle and Repeat buttons yet again. Open the Now Playing screen, tap on the new Up Next button next to the AirPlay button to spot the Shuffle and Repeat buttons at the top (highlighted in the screenshot above).

Create Memoji From Any iPhone

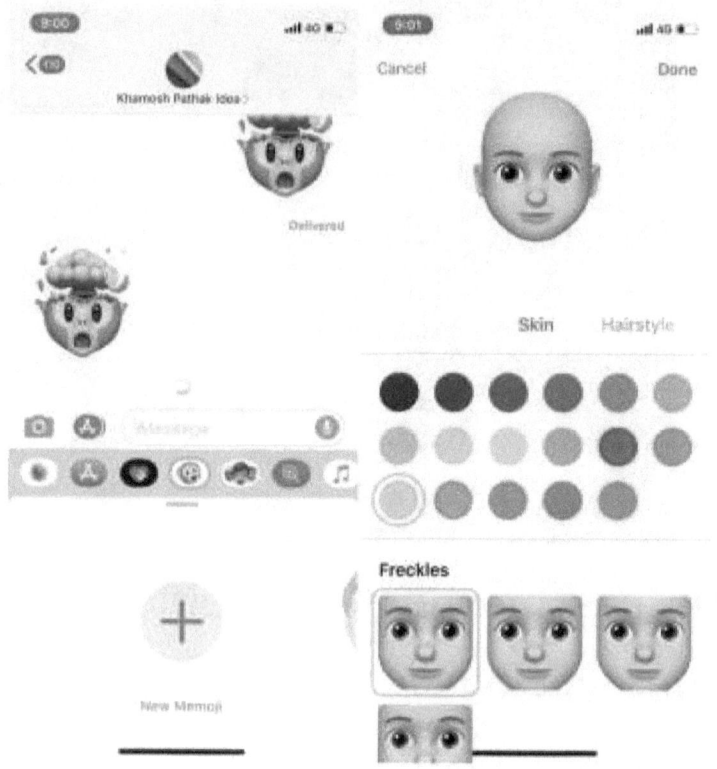

Any iPhone with an A9 processor or higher can create a Memoji. Open the Messages app, click on the Animoji icon, swipe left and tap on the New button to start customizing your Memoji.

Set Your Custom iMessage Profile

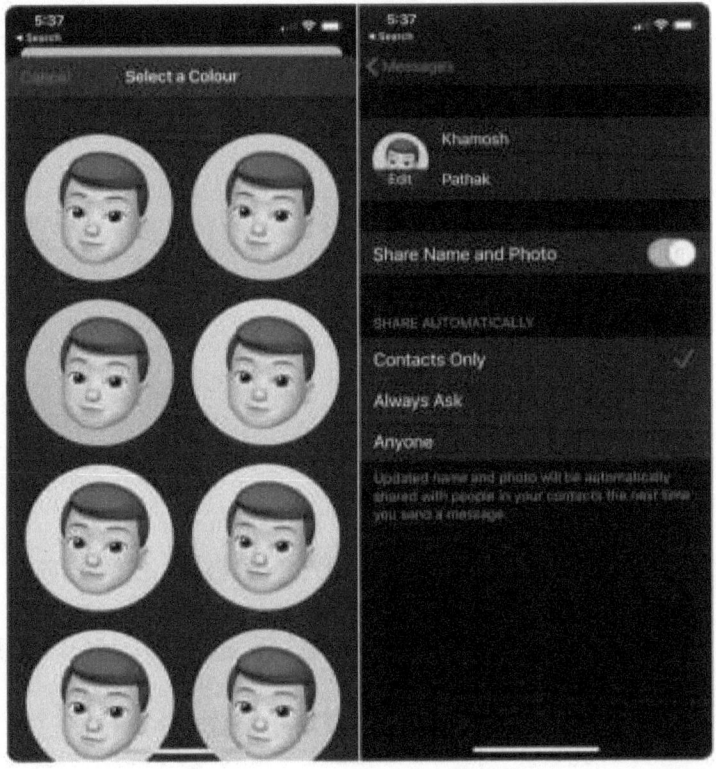

You can now set a custom iMessage profile with a separate name and a photo and you can choose who to share it with. Go to Settings -> Messages -> Share Name and Photo to set it up. Next, select if you want to share with Contacts Only, Anyone or Always Ask.

Use Memoji Stickers Anywhere in iOS

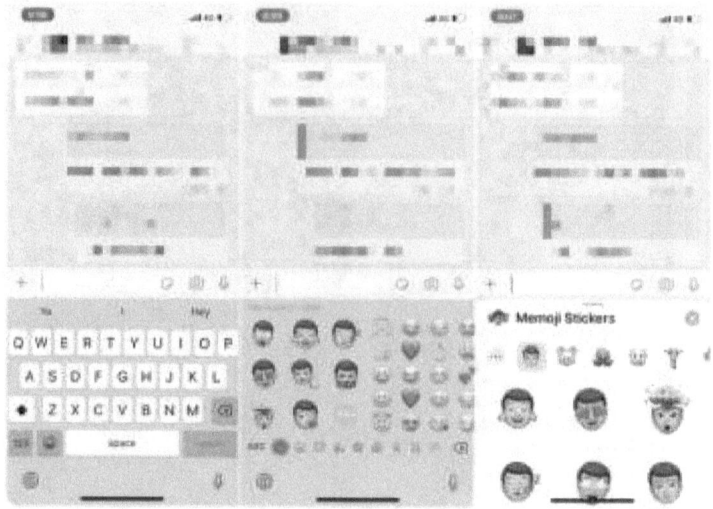

Once you create a Memoji avatar, Apple will automatically create a sticker pack for you. This will be available in the new iMessage app called Animoji Stickers. But the best part is that they can be accessed from anywhere in iOS using the Emoji keyboard.

Automatically Close Tabs in Safari

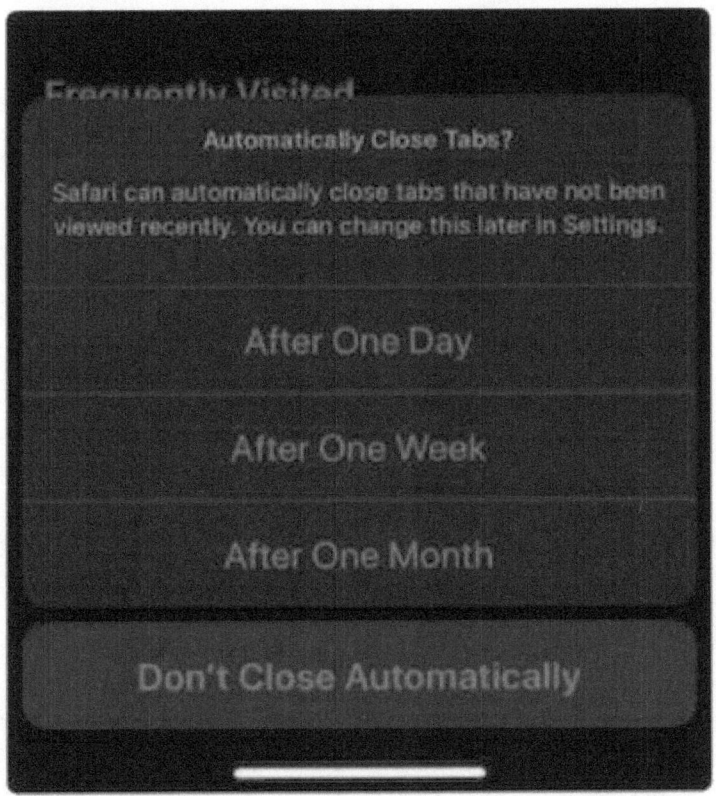

There's now a feature to automatically close unused Safari tabs after a set time. You'll get this option when you try to close all tabs together. You can set this up manually by going to Settings -> Safari -> Close Tabs.

Toggle Wi-Fi and Bluetooth From Control Center

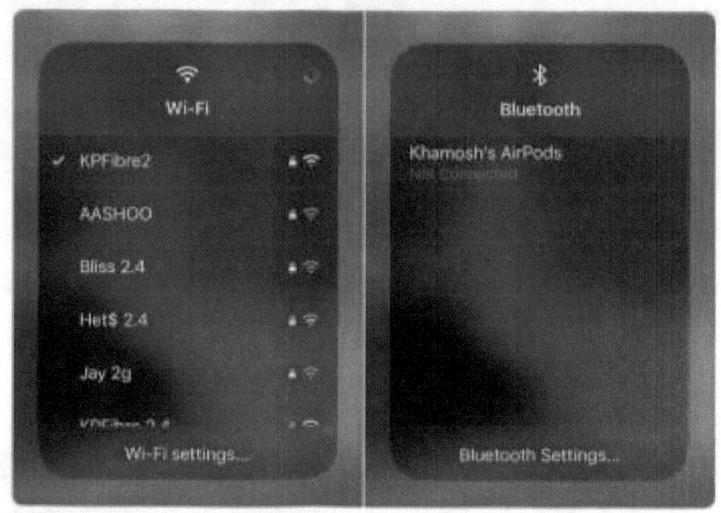

If you press and hold the Wi-Fi or Bluetooth toggles in Control Center you'll be able to switch between available networks or directly open the Settings section.

Download Large Apps over Cellular

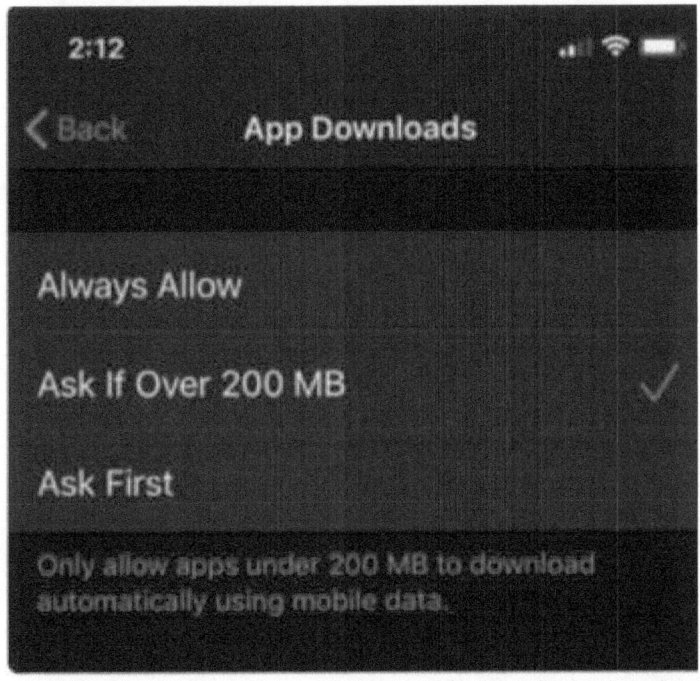

Apple has removed the 200MB limit for app downloads over a cellular network. Now when you try to download a big app over cellular, you'll be asked if you really want to go ahead. And you can disable the prompt forever by going to Settings -> iTunes & App Store -> App Downloads.

Use External Storage With Files App

You can connect a USB drive or an SD Card reader to an iPhone using a converter cable to access all the files right there.

Scan Documents in Files App

Tap the Menu button at the top of the Files app to see a new Scan Documents feature. This works similar to how it does in the Notes app.

Use Haptic Touch on Every iPhone

Users as far back as iPhone SE are now able to access features like the Home screen app quick actions. What used to show up when a user would 3D Touch an element, now shows up with just a tap and hold (with haptic feedback).

Silence Unknown Callers

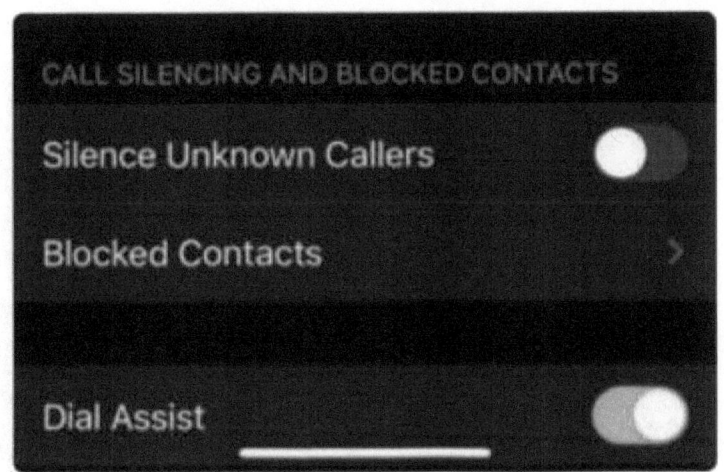

This new option in Settings will automatically silence calls from callers who are not in your Contacts app, Messages app or Mail app. The call will automatically go to your Voicemail. You can then go in later and listen to the message to see if it was important. If you're using Visual Voicemail, you can read the text transcript to judge. Go to Settings -> Messages -> Silence Unknown Callers to enable it.

Optimize Battery Charging

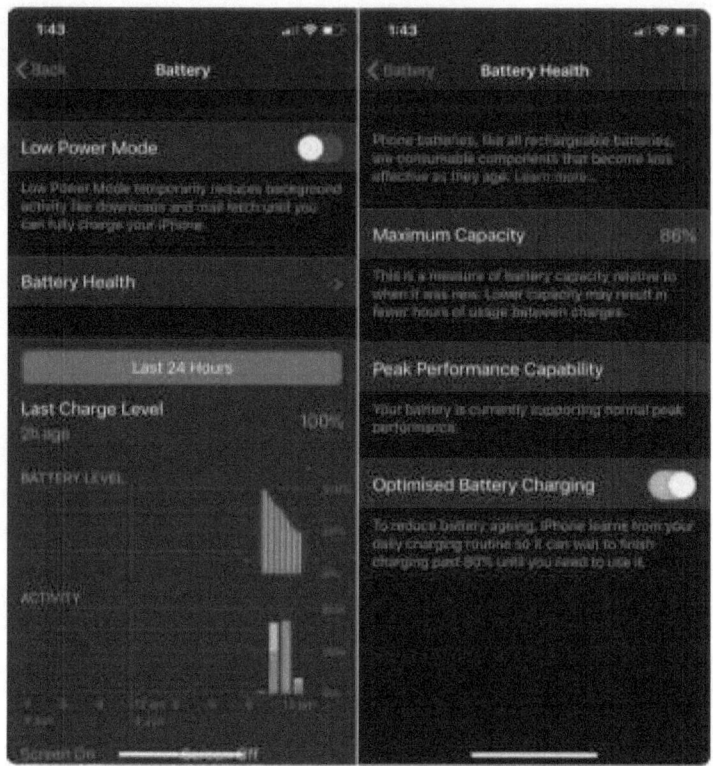

There's a new option in Battery Health called Optimized Battery Charging. This helps reduce battery aging. The iPhone learns from your daily charging routine so it can wait to finish charging past 80% until you need to use it.

Find The New Updates Section in App Store

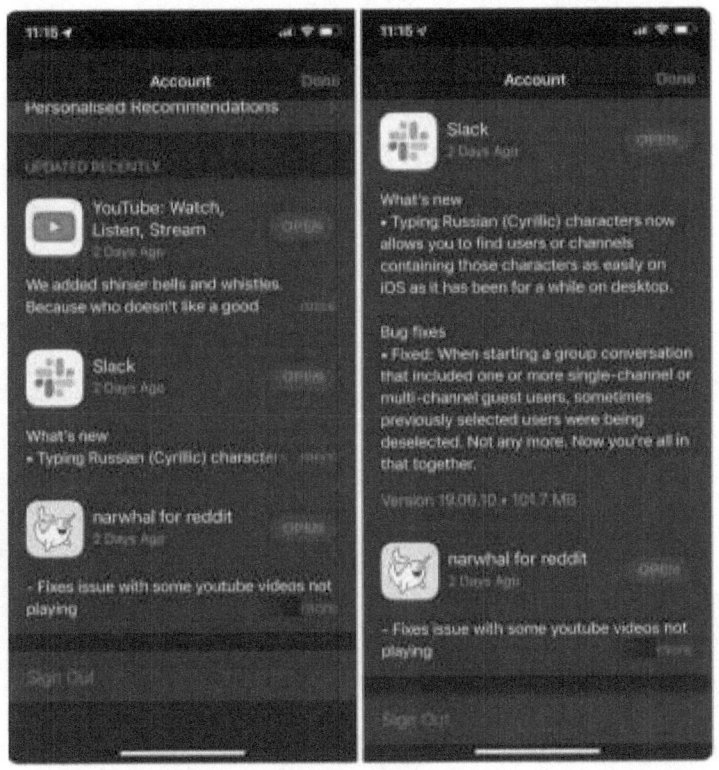

Updates section has been moved in the iOS 13 update. Instead of the Updates tab, you'll find the Arcade tab. To locate the Updates section go to the Today tab and tap on your Profile icon. You'll see the updates in the bottom section.

Delete Apps From Updates Section

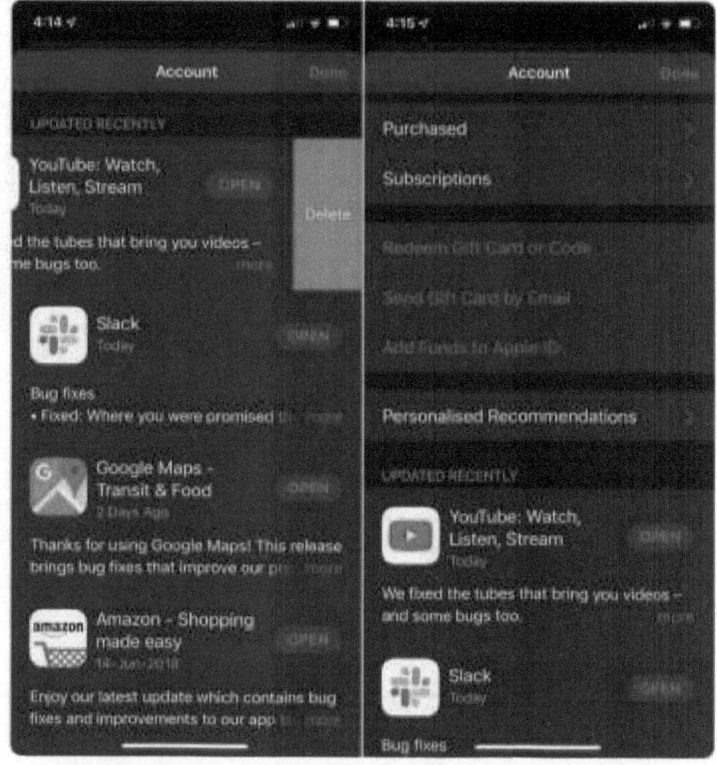

You can now swipe Left on an update listing to delete the app from your iPhone.

Use Automatic Dark Mode for Supported Websites in Safari

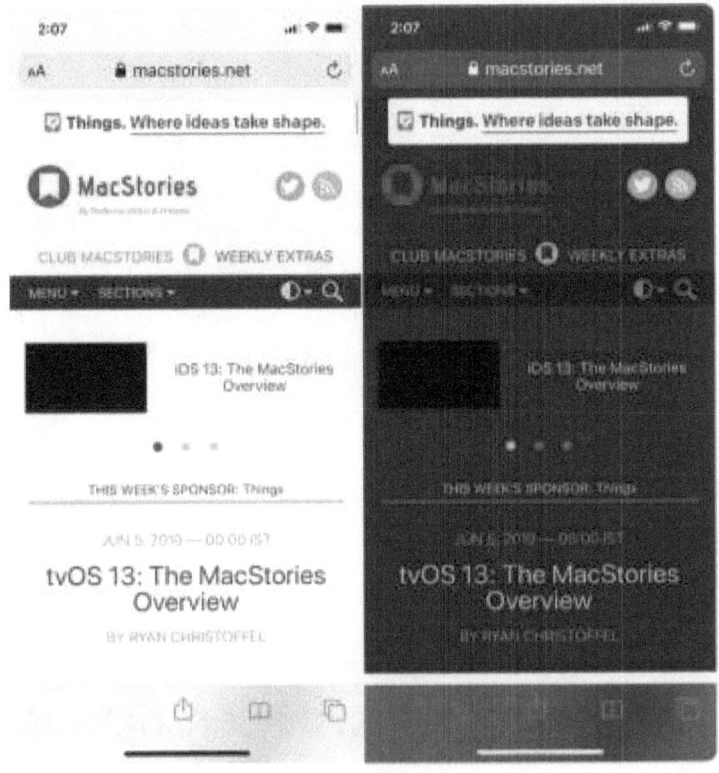

Safari on iOS has an experimental feature called Dark Mode CSS Support. This means that if a website has special CSS code pertaining to Dark mode it will automatically load that version of the site when the iOS device is in dark mode.

Create Real Automations in Shortcuts

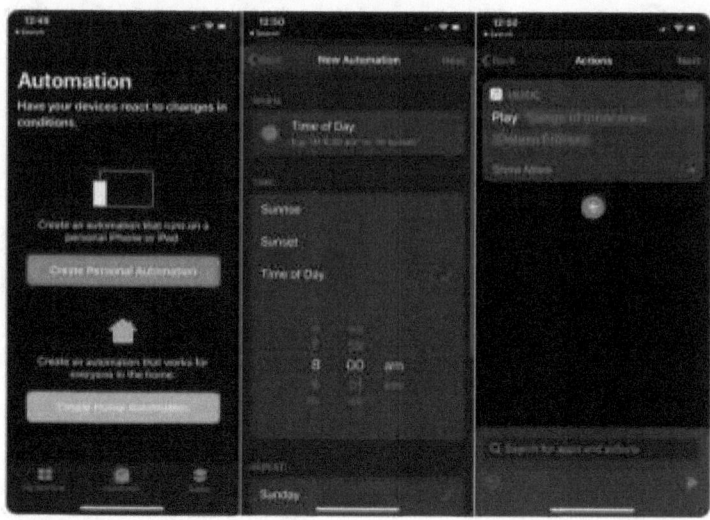

Shortcuts app in iOS 13 now supports real automations. You can now create shortcuts that get triggered using an array of options. It can be based on a time, when you open an app, using NFC tags, and more. Go to the new Automation tab in Shortcuts app and tap on the Plus button to get started.

Use The Better Formatting Features in Mail App

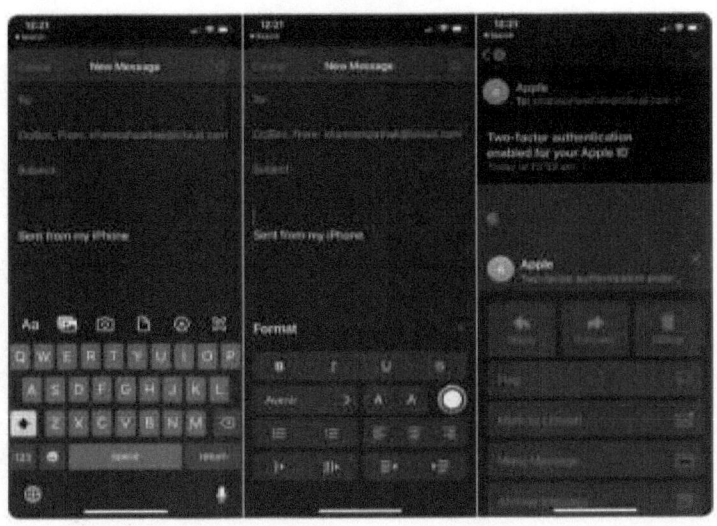

Mail app now has desktop-class formatting options in iOS 13. Tap on the compose box and then tap on the Left Arrow icon to bring in the new toolbar. Tap on the Aa icon to view the formatting feature. From here, you can change the font, font size, font style, indentation, and more.

Save All Open Tabs as Bookmarks in Safari

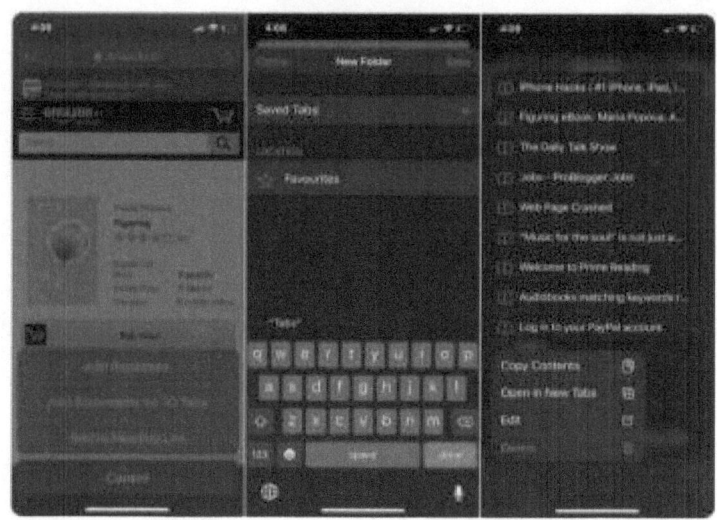

There's a new option in Safari to quickly save all open tabs as bookmarks. Tap and hold on the Bookmarks button to get the Add Bookmarks For N Tabs option. All bookmarks will be saved in one folder and can all be opened together as well.

Zip and unzip Files in Files App

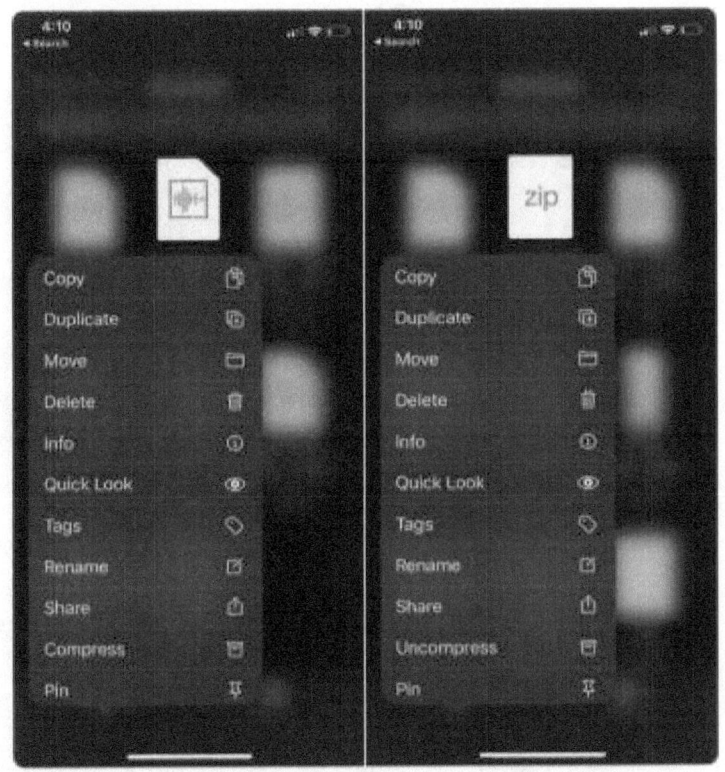

If you tap and hold on a zip file in Files app, you'll find the Uncompress option to quickly unzip it. You can also compress a file, a folder or multiple files in the same way.

Organize Files and Folders in Local Storage

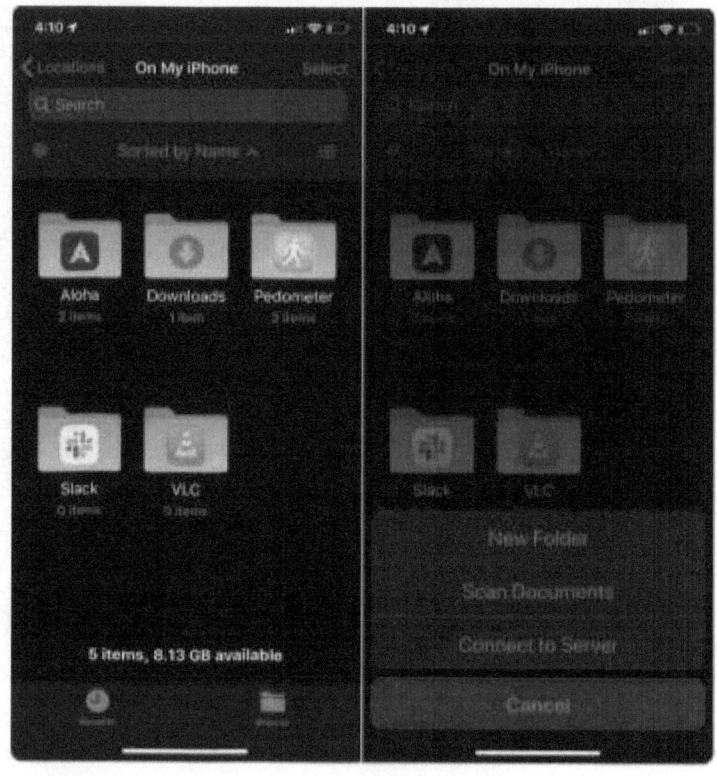

Local Storage in Files app can now be manipulated by the user. You can create folders, move files around without involving iCloud Drive.

Take Full Page Screenshots in Safari

When you take a screenshot in Safari and tap on the preview box, you'll see a new Full Page option at the top. Tap on it and you'll be able to mark up and capture the entire page.

Use Low Data Mode for Specific Wi-Fi Networks

Go to a Wi-Fi network's info page and you'll spot a new Low Data mode option. When you turn it on.

Quickly Open Emojis With The New Dedicated Button

On the iPhone X and higher, the Keyboard Switcher icon has been moved to the empty space below the keyboard. There's a new dedicated Emoji button in the bottom row which you can use to quickly switch in and out of the Emoji keyboard.

Use Shortcuts Directly From Share Sheet

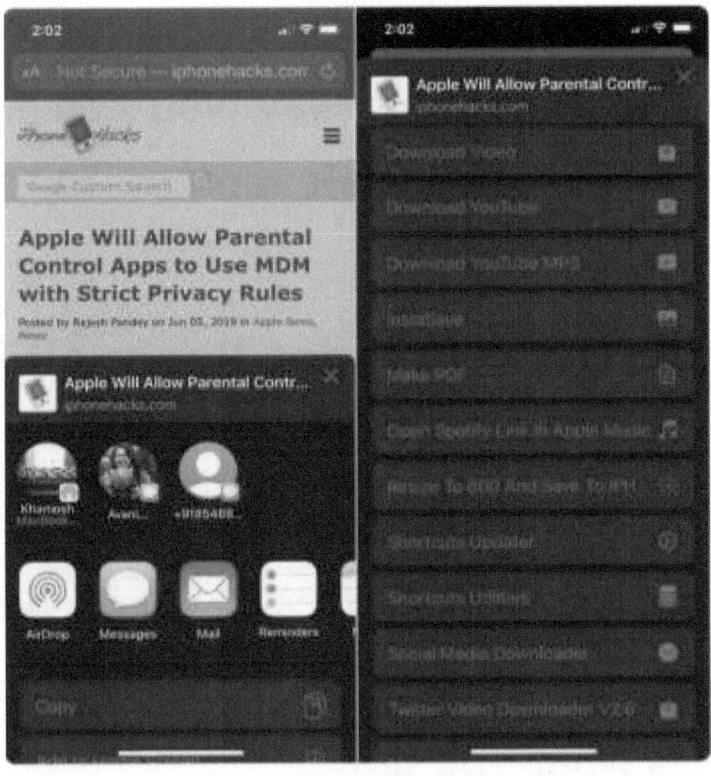

This is one of the advantages of Shortcuts app being built into the OS. You'll now see relevant shortcuts for the app in the

Actions list in the Share sheet. Saves an extra step.

Save Screenshots to Files App Instead

When you try to save a screenshot from the preview, you'll get a new option called Save to Files. This way you can save an annotated screenshot directly to a folder in Files.

Mute Those Dreaded Reply-All Email Threads

If you get trapped in an awful Reply All email thread that's blowing up your phone, don't fret — you can escape! Here's what you do:

- Open your Mail app on your iPhone
- In your inbox, swipe right to left across the message

- Tap More

- Tape Mute

- If you want to rejoin the conversation, repeat the first three steps, but tap Unmute

Use Siri to Play Live Radio

In iOS 13, you can ask Siri to play your favorite radio stations. Here's what you ask your assistant:

- Activate Siri by holding the power button or with a "Hey Siri" command

- Say "Siri, play radio station (name of radio station) ."

- Rock out!

Type Faster by Swiping

Swipe-style keyboards have been popular on Android devices for a while now. It wasn't until a few months ago that Apple allowed users to install third-party keyboards like Gboard to add the functionality. Now you don't have to even have to go to the App Store to install one.

If you want to use Apple's new QuickPath typing just install iOS 13, then compose a message like you normally would. To "type," drag and hold your finger or thumb on each letter of the word you're trying to spell. This may take some time getting used to.

How To Create Nested Subtasks in iOS 13's Reminders App for More Organized To-Do Lists

Things are a bit more organized in Apple Reminders, so the cluttered mess that it once was is no more in iOS 13. The slapped-together feel in older iOS versions was the main reason I never used it that much, but the updated version for iPhone has finally got me hooked.

Aside from being able to create grouped lists, which are folders that contain several lists within them, you can also nest reminders in a list underneath other reminders. Having main tasks and subtasks does a lot for organization and makes the structure obvious with just a glance.

For example, in a shopping list, you may be at the grocery store looking for ingredients for different recipes or meals. Now, instead of creating separate lists for each dish or having all of the ingredients haphazardly combined, you can make the dish a parent with subtasks (ingredients) underneath it. And there are a few ways to create the parent and subtask reminders, depending on how you're starting.

Note that you can only make subtasks for lists in your iCloud account, not on third-party services such as Yahoo or Outlook. At least, not yet.

Option 1 - Drag & Drop Subtasks onto a Parent Reminder

If you already have reminders in the list you want to convert to subtasks for another reminder, press-and-hold on one one of them, then drag and drop it on top of the reminder you want to be the parent. The parent reminder will bold itself, indicating itself as the main task, and the subtask will be indented below it.

Repeat that process for any other tasks you want to move under the parent. It seems like you may be able to bulk move subtasks in the future, similar to how you would bulk-move app icons on the home screen, but it's not entirely working yet.

To remove a subtask, you can drag and drop it out of the parent reminder into its own spot in the list or another parent directory. Aside from checking it off as complete, you can also delete it by short-swiping left and hitting "Delete," or long-swiping left to do it automatically.

With a short-swipe left, there's also an option to "Flag" it, which will add a little flag icon next to it and add it to the automated "Flagged" section on the main screen. You can short-swipe left again and hit "Unflag" to remove the flag.

Option 2 - Indent Subtasks into a Parent Reminder

Another way to create subtasks for a parent reminder, if you already have reminders you want to convert in the list, is to indent them. First, drag and drop all of the reminders you want to be subtasks, so they are situated below the one you want to make a parent. Next, for the reminders you want to make subtasks, short-swipe right on them and hit "Indent" or long-swipe right to indent automatically.

It doesn't matter what order you go in when indenting. For instance, if you indent the first subtask under the parent, then the second, and so on, they'll all be subtasks of the parent. If you indent the last subtask first, it will become a subtask for whatever subtask was above it. But indenting that "parent" wannabe will make it and its subtasks as subtasks of the next reminder above, and you can do this until you reach the real parent.

To remove a subtask with the indent method, short-swipe right on it and hit "Outdent," or long-swipe on it to outdent it automatically. If you outdent a subtask somewhere in between other subtasks in the parent directory, that outdented subtask will become its own parent with everything that was underneath now subtasks for it instead of the original parent.

To rearrange, flag, or delete subtasks, you can do so just as described in Option 1.

Option 3 - Add New Subtasks from a Parent Reminder's Details

If you don't already have subtasks in the current list, it's easier to create them from inside the parent reminder directly. So either create a "New Reminder" to be the parent or tap on a reminder in the list already that you want to be the parent. Next, tap on its information (i) icon to open its Details modal view. Tap on "Subtasks" near the bottom, then "Add

Reminder" for each subtask you want to create.

To make sure newly added subtasks are saved, hit the "return" or "enter" key on the keyboard or hit "Add Reminder" again after typing one out. That will pop you into a new bubble for the next subtask to add.

If you add a subtask you didn't want, edit it to something else or short-swipe left on it and hit "Delete," or long-swipe left to remove it automatically. When no more subtasks are needed, tap "Details" to go back. While you can't flag all of the subtasks from the parent's Details page, you can toggle on "Flagged" to flag the parent. Doing so won't flag all the subtasks underneath, only the parent.

Toggle it back off to unflag it. Hit "Done" to finalize things.

View & Hide Nested Reminders

Tap on the chevron to the right of the parent reminder to either view or hide the nested reminders. When hidden, a number in the parent reminder will show you how many subtasks there are. Plus, it helps de-clutter the list, so you only see individual   reminders   and parent reminders.

Flag & Delete Parent Reminders

To flag or delete a subtask or parent reminder, short-swipe left on it, then hit "Flag" or "Deleted." You can also long-swipe   left   on   one   to   delete   it automatically. If you delete a regular reminder, subtask, or parent directory, it will do it right away — there is not a confirmation prompt. And if you delete a parent, all subtasks within will also go poof.

How To Use a Wireless or USB Mouse on Your iPhone in iOS 13

For the first time, you can officially use a computer mouse with your iPhone, thanks to Apple's new Accessibility settings in iOS 13. It works for all types of Bluetooth mice, so if you have one, it'll already work. Plus, those with wireless receivers and even wired mice are supported by using a USB to Lightning adapter.

There are many benefits to using a mouse pointer, and the most significant one is because of difficulty using a touchscreen device with your fingers. It's particularly tricky using touch when it's hard to accurately tell what you're tapping or if your fingers are relatively large. With a mouse, there is no obscurement of the display.

Additionally, you can hover a pointer on the screen to highlight something for someone or to help follow along when reading. It can be faster to perform actions in some scenarios. There's more precision. It's great to have when your display isn't registering touches correctly. And you'll likely be able to play games faster and better.

Step 1 - Open the Pointing Options

The feature in iOS 13 is hiding in the Accessibility menu, which has changed places since iOS 12. To access it and the mouse settings, open the Settings app, tap "Accessibility," then "Touch" under Physical and Motor.

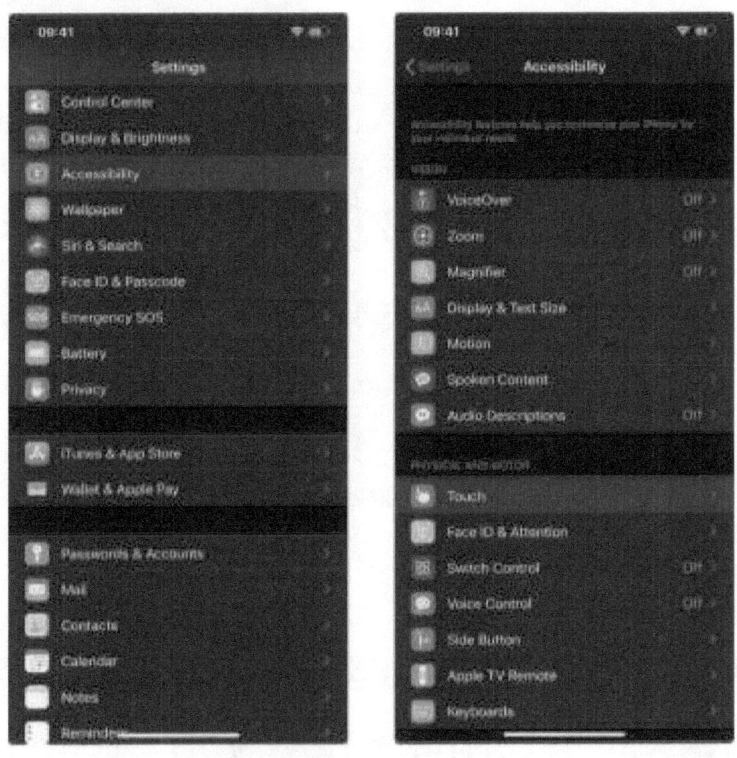

Next, tap "AssistiveTouch" up top, then "Devices" under Pointer Devices.

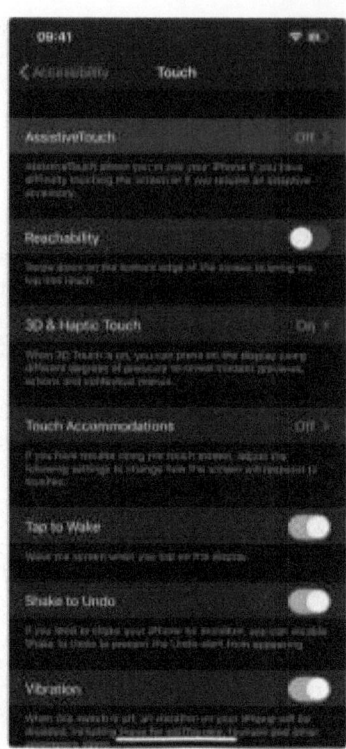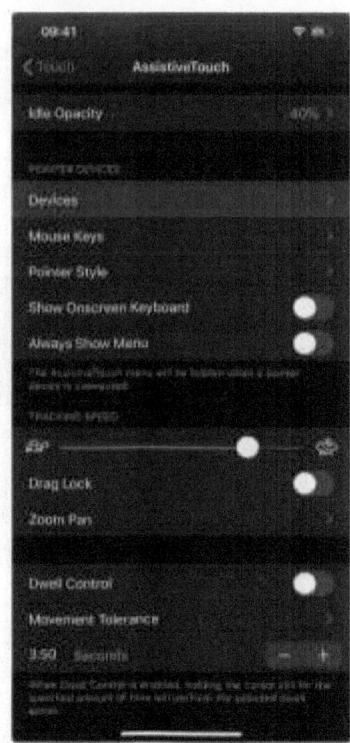

Step 2 - Pair Your Computer Mouse

The type of wireless computer mouse you have will determine how you set it up, but both ways are easy. However, if you have a Bluetooth mouse without any dongles, you may have an easier time using the mouse since we've found that mice with USB dongle receivers are forgotten relatively quickly by the iPhone.

Option 1 - Pairing a Bluetooth Mouse Without a USB Receiver

Make sure Bluetooth is enabled on your iPhone, as well as your Bluetooth mouse. If this is your first time pairing a mouse with your iPhone, the "Devices" menu's only option will be "Bluetooth Devices." Tap that, then on the name of your discovered mouse once it appears.

Then, just tap "Pair" on the Bluetooth Pairing Request pop-up, and you're done. Go back a screen, and you'll see your mouse listed under the new Connected Devices section. Once connected, move on to Step 3 below.

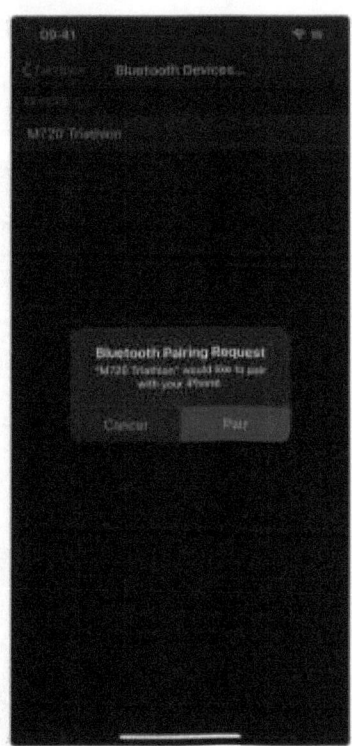 

Alternatively, you can navigate away to the "Bluetooth" options in the Settings app (you'll be going back to the AssistiveTouch settings later). Look for the mouse in the My Devices section. Tap on it to "Pair" it with your iPhone. Once connected, move on to Step 3 below.

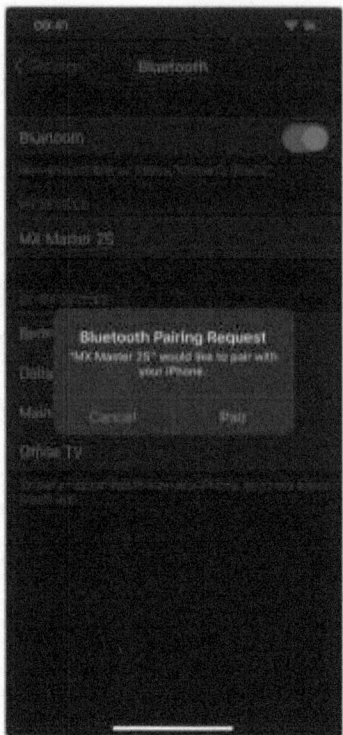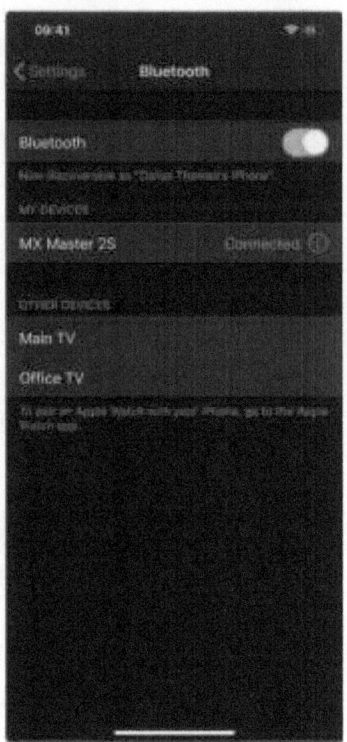

Option 2 - Pairing a Wired or Wireless Mouse with USB Receiver

On the "Devices" page, you will see the "Bluetooth Devices" option, but that's not what you want. That's only for mice that connect via Bluetooth. For the ones with USB-based receivers or wired ones, you'll need to have a USB to Lightning adapter. If you've used our guide on transferring photos and videos from a DSLR camera to your iPhone, you likely have one ready to go.

If you don't have an adapter, you will need to get Apple's Lightning to USB Camera Adapter ($29) or Lightning to USB 3 Camera Adapter ($39). Either of these will work, but the cheaper one is good enough for use with your computer mouse.

When you have one, make sure your mouse is turned on, then connect the USB receiver or USB cable for the mouse to the USB end of the adapter. Next, plug in the adapter to the iPhone's Lightning port. Immediately, you should see an option appear for "USB Receiver" under Connected Devices. Tap that, then proceed to Step 3.

Step 3 - Customize Your Mouse Clicks

No matter what type of computer mouse you have, after you select it in the "Devices" menu (go back there if you paired the mouse from the Settings app), you'll have options to customize what buttons do what. Depending on your mouse, some buttons may already be assigned. On a three-button mouse, the defaults seem to be "Single-Tap" for the left-click, "Open Menu" for the right-click, and "Home" for scroll-click. You can tap any of these buttons and change the action to something different.

All of the actions include None, Single-Tap, Open Menu, 3D Touch (if your iPhone supports it), Accessibility Shortcut, Analytics, App Switcher, Control Center, Double Tap, Home, Lock Rotation, Lock Screen, Long Press, Mute, Notifications, Pinch, Reachability, Restart, Screenshot, Shake, Siri, SOS, Speak Screen, Spotlight, Voice Control, Volume Down, Volume Up, and Apple Pay.

Additionally, you can assign any button to any of your Siri Shortcuts.

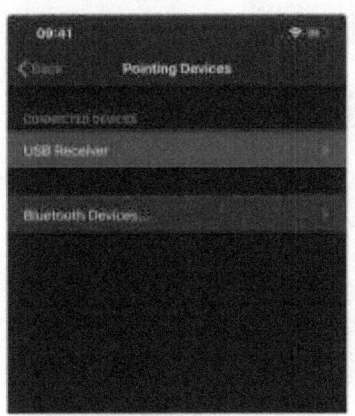 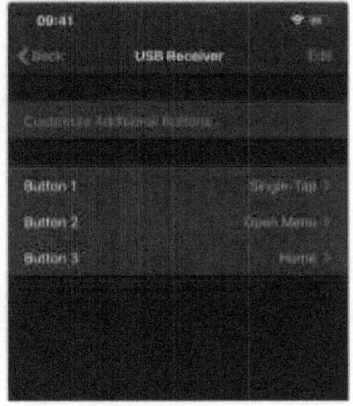

If you don't see any buttons already available to set up, or if not all of your mouse's buttons are present, you can force your iPhone to recognize the other buttons. To do so, tap "Customize Additional Buttons" at the top. A prompt will appear asking you to press a button on your pointing device to choose an action. When you do, the button should appear in the list which you could associate with any of the available options seen above.

Step 4 - Use the Computer Mouse on Your iPhone

Now for the big moment — actually using the mouse with your iPhone. Since this is an AssistiveTouch feature, you need to turn AssistiveTouch on. So back out of the Devices settings until you're on the AssistiveTouch screen again, then toggle on "AssistiveTouch" at the top. Alternatively, you can use the triple-click Home or Side button shortcut if you have that enabled for AssistiveTouch.

The circular AssistiveTouch menu icon will appear, as well as the circular mouse cursor. You can disable the AssistiveTouch icon when a pointer is active by toggling off "Always Show Menu" in the AssistiveTouch settings.

Depending on what actions you chose for each button, mouse use will vary from person to person. But if you stuck with the defaults as I did above, left-clicking will select things. Left-clicking and holding it down will grab items or let you perform swipes like to open the Control Center or Notification Center.

Right-clicking will open the AssistiveTouch menu. And clicking the middle button will take you to the home screen. It's relatively intuitive and easy to use — just like a mouse on your computer.

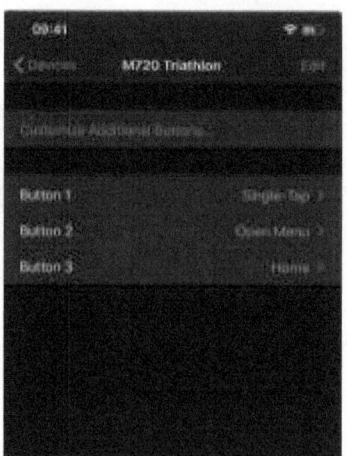 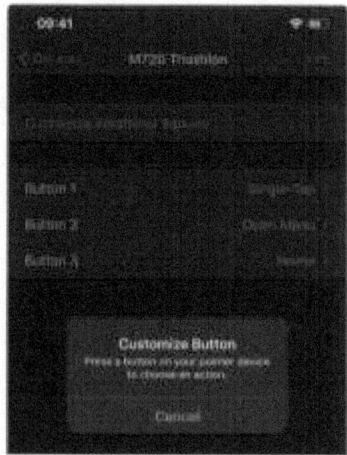

Step 5 - Change the Tracking Speed of the Cursor (Optional)

I found that the cursor was going too fast on the screen, so I had to turn the tracking speed down. If you're in a similar situation, or if your cursor is moving too slow on the screen, you can adjust it. In the same AssistiveTouch menu, find the Tracking Speed section. In it, there's a slider which you can adjust — left toward the turtle slows it down, right toward the rabbit speeds it up.

Step 6 - Change the Cursor Size, Color & Visibility (Optional)

If you're using iOS 13's new Dark Mode feature, the default gray color of the cursor may be hard to see, but you can change it. In the AssistiveTouch menu, tap on "Pointer Style" Then, select "Color," where you'll find options for gray, white, blue, red, green, yellow, and orange.

Back in the "Pointer Style" menu, there are options to choose the how big the circular cursor is under the Size section. There are ten available cursor sizes on the slider. Also, you can tap "Auto-Hide" to disable the feature to see the cursor always or to change the amount of time the cursor will hide after.

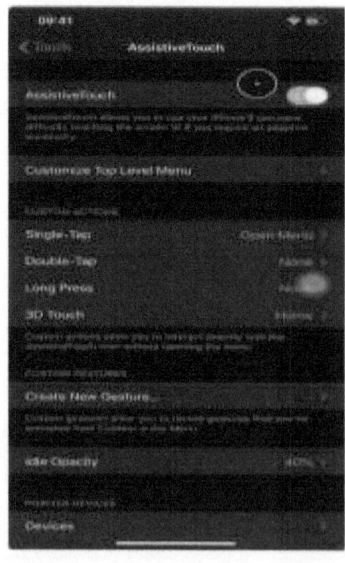 

Step 7 - Enable Drag Lock for Scrolling (Optional)

By default, when you left-click-and-hold, then move the mouse up or down on a page, it will let you scroll. Let go, and it acts just like your finger was removed from the screen, and if you want to scroll more, repeat the process. When you left-click-and-hold for one second, release, then move the mouse, the pointer just moves.

However, you can lock the cursor to the place where you left-clicked-and-held, so you can only scroll up and down as much as the cursor can appear on the screen. To try this out, turn on the "Drag Lock" toggle in the AssistiveTouch menu. Then, left-click-and-hold somewhere on a page, give it a second, release the button, then move the mouse around, and you'll immediately notice the cursor "locked" to that spot on the page. To get rid of the lock, just left-click to disable it.

Without the drag locked (left) and with it locked (right).

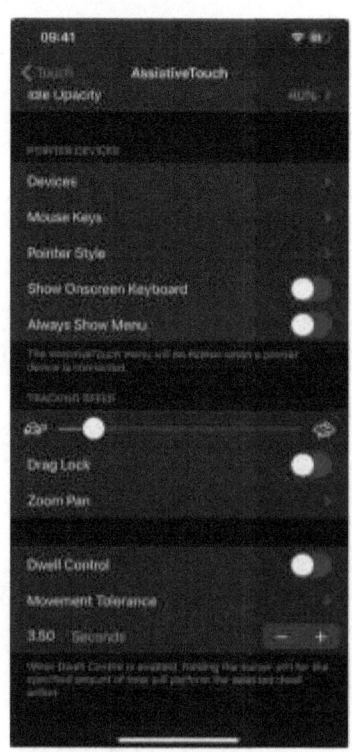 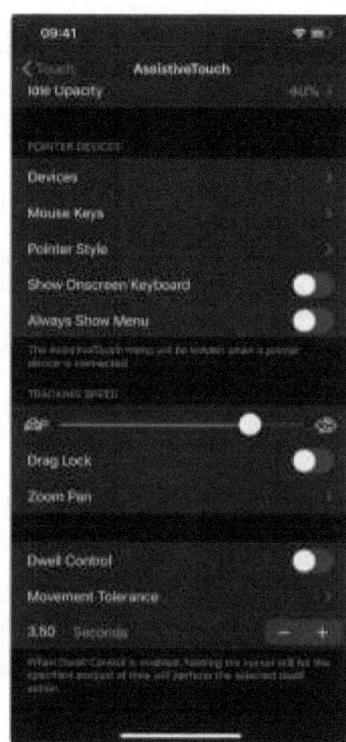

Step 8 - Adjust the Zoom Pan Options (Optional)

If you use the "Zoom" feature at all with your iPhone, this is an excellent setting to check out. In the AssistiveTouch options in the Tracking Speed section, tap on "Zoom Pan." There are three options to choose from:

- **Continuous**: When zoomed in, the screen will always move with the cursor.

- **Centered**: When zoomed in, the cursor will stay in the middle of the screen with the page moving accordingly.

- **Edges**: When zoomed in, the screen only moves when the cursor

moves   around   the   edges   of
the display.

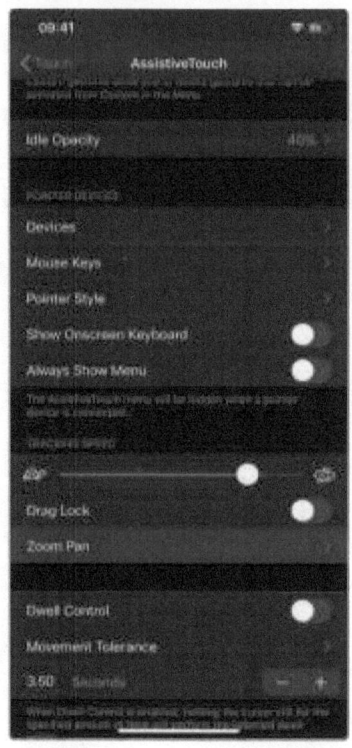 

Step 9 - Enable the Dwell Setting (Optional)

If you don't like clicking at all, you can minimize it with the "Dwell Control" setting in the AssistiveTouch menu. Toggle it on, and whenever you hover over something on the screen, and in a few seconds, it will perform that action for you. Note: with this option enabled, the AssistiveTouch menu icon needs to be on, and it will turn it on automatically for you.

You can adjust the time frame for when the action will be initiated, so if you're hovering over a menu icon, you can change how long the hover is before it will open that menu icon up. Use the plus and minus signs next to "Seconds" to adjust it from 0.25 seconds to 4.25 seconds in 0.25-second increments.

The "Movement Tolerance" setting provides a slider you can adjust for the distance you can move while dwelling on an item. Move beyond the limit, and the action won't happen. Sliding the white dot left decreases the radius while moving right increases the radius.

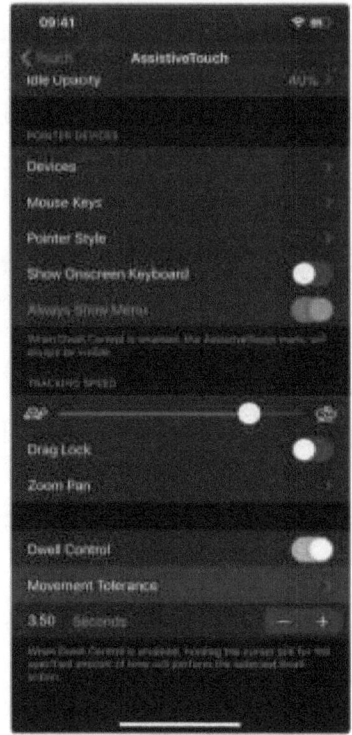

So far, this is an excellent attempt at incorporating computer mice into iOS. It's likely more useful in iPadOS 13 since you can use that as a real computer, but it's still beneficial on iPhone. However, there's one thing I wish were included in the pointer settings — a way to change how the scroll wheel works.

To me, it's unnatural the way scrolling works in the "natural" setting, similar to the natural setting on macOS, but it may not be to you. When scrolling on the iPhone, when you scroll the wheel toward you, the page scrolls up, and scrolling the wheel away makes it scroll down. I prefer the approach where scrolling the wheel toward you makes the page scroll down, and away makes it go up.

Enable Dark Mode

One of the most anticipated features of iOS 13 is Dark Mode. If you're unfamiliar, the setting essentially inverts the colors on your screen, so all the white background interfaces turn black. This lets your eyes rest easier at nighttime. It also just looks really cool. Here's how you turn it on!

- Just say, "Hey, Siri, turn on Dark Mode"
- If you prefer not to use Siri, you can open Control Center by swiping down diagonally on the top-right corner of your iPhone's display
- Press and hold the Brightness indicator (it looks like a sun)
- Tap Appearance Light at the bottom left

That's it!

Change Your Profile Picture

If you want to have a profile picture for when your friends add your info to their contacts, here's how you set a default profile picture.

- Open your Messages app

- Tap the ••• button on the right of your screen

- Select Edit Name and Photo

- Tap on the profile icon to change your image.

- You can snap a photo using the Camera, upload a photo from your photo library, or you can even use an Animoji or Memoji instead.

Track Your Menstrual Cycle

The Health app in iOS 13 now offers a way for women to track important data about their menstrual cycle. You can log your period, flow level, and any symptoms like cramps or headaches, and whether or not you have experienced spotting. The feature also offers predictions as to when your cycle may begin and end for the next three cycles. Here's how you can start using the tool:

- Open the Health app on your iPhone
- Tap the Search tab at the bottom right of your screen
- Select Cycle Tracking
- Tap Options to start inputting information

Change Wi-Fi Networks Faster

If you're tired of opening up the Settings app to connect to Wi-Fi hotspots, you should know there's a faster way!

- Open Control Center by swiping down diagonally on the top-right corner of your iPhone's display.

- Tap and hold your finger on the middle of the Wi-Fi widget

- Press and hold your finger on Wi-Fi bars icon to see a list of available networks

- This trick also works for pairing Bluetooth devices!

Silence Unknown Callers

Kiss robocalls goodbye with this must-install trick.

- Open the Settings app
- Tap Phone
- Toggle Silence Unknown Callers

Automatically Close Browser Tabs

As scary as this tip may sound, it's actually quite useful and helps keep your web browser running more efficiently. This trick only works for the default Safari internet browser.

- Open your Settings app
- Tap Safari
- Tap Close Tabs
- You can set it to close your tabs each day, each week, every month, or leave it on manual mode.

Prolong Your iPhone Battery

Apple has added a new option to its Battery Health feature called "Optimized Battery Charging," which is designed to extend the total battery life of a device running iOS 13. Apple says the feature slows the rate of battery aging by reducing the time your iPhone spends fully charged. The tool uses machine learning to understand your daily charging routine, so it can wait to finish charging past 80% until you need to use your phone. That way if you charge your phone at night, it won't hold a 100% charge for several hours, which degrades your battery.

- Tap Settings
- Scroll down
- Tap Battery
- Tap Battery Health
- Toggle the switch to the On position.

Start a Group FaceTime Call

You've probably FaceTimed a million times with your family and friends, but have you ever FaceTimed several of them simultaneously? Here's how:

- Open the FaceTime app on your iPhone
- Tap the + button on the top right of your screen
- Enter the name or number of the person you want to call first
- Enter up to 30 additional contacts
- Tap Video or Audio to place your FaceTime call

Access the Calculator Faster

If you need to do math on the fly but don't want to open the calculator app, there's a faster way you didn't know about!

- Swipe right over the home screen, lock screen, or while you're looking at your notifications
- Type in the operation
- Your iPhone will calculate it for you

This piece of advice will definitely come in handy when you need to figure out the tip at a restaurant.

Extend Battery Life Easily

There's a setting on your iPhone called "Low Power Mode" that you may not know about. It reduces power consumption by turning off a number of battery draining features like dimming the screen faster, retrieving email less frequently, and turning off background app refresh. Here's how you can turn it on so you can get more battery life:

- Open the Settings app
- Tap "Battery"
- Enable Low Power Mode

Make Your iPhone Flash When You Get a Notification

If you'd rather have a visual cue over an auditory one, you should know that your iPhone's LED light can actually flash anytime you get pinged. Just make sure you don't have the setting on at a theater! Here's how you can turn the setting on:

- Open your settings app
- Tap "General"
- Tap "Accessibility"
- Scroll down a little bit
- Tap "Enable LED Flash for Alerts"

Take More Level, Better-Framed Photos

There's a hidden camera level deep in the iPhone's settings that'll come in handy for when you're taking overhead shots of your stuff. To turn the feature on go to:

- Settings
- Scroll down some
- Tap "Camera"
- Enable the Grid

When you hold your phone over something to take a photo, two crosshairs will appear — a white one and a yellow one. When they line up, your photo is level!

How To Disable Message Effects from Auto-Playing on Your iPhone

Message effects in iMessage lets you add a touch of flair to otherwise bland communications. With the feature, you can complement a birthday wish with a stream of balloons, send a congratulatory text along with a shower of confetti, or make the chat bubble slam itself in the thread. If you're on the receiving end, however, they may be distracting and even jarring.

According to Apple, one in three people have some degree of motion sensibility, which mostly applies to car rides and boat trips. But a small subset of those people can be triggered from mere motion effects or movement on a smartphone screen.

If you're one of those users, you can disable message effects from playing in Messages without your approval. Even if you aren't affected by screen movement, disabling auto-playing effects will keep distractions to a minimum to help you read texts faster and go back to the rest of your day.

The process differs depending on what iOS version you're running. If you're running iOS 10, 11, or 12, it will be the same method, but things change in iOS 13 since the Accessibility menu is in a different location.

Method 1 - Disable iMessage Screen Effects in iOS 13

Open up the Settings app, then go to Accessibility -> Motion. There, you'll see a menu item called "Auto-Play Message Effects." Toggle that off, and messages effects, whether they are bubble effects or screen effects, should not play right away. Best of all, you don't need to enable "Reduce Motion" for it to stop playing message effects.

Method 2 - Disable iMessage Screen Effects in iOS 10–12

Open up the Settings app, then go to General   -> Accessibility   -> Reduce Motion. Next, make sure "Reduce

Motion" is toggled on, then disable the toggle for "Auto-Play Message Effects" underneath it. Now, messages effects, whether they are bubble effects or screen effects, should not play right away.

No matter which iOS version you're running, when "Auto-Play Message Effects" is disabled, incoming messages will come in without any message effects. That means no Slam, Loud, Gentle, or Invisible Ink bubbles, nor any Echo, Spotlight, Balloons, Confetti, Love, Lasers, Fireworks, Shooting Star, or Celebration screen effects.

If you do want to view them, there will be a "Replay [Effect]" under the message. Tapping that will play them as they were meant to be seen, so they only play when you want them to play. It is worth noting, however, that any messages you send with effects will play the effects for you when you hit the send button, regardless as to whether "Auto-Play Message Effects" is on or off. The setting only affects incoming messages.

Stop Apps from Asking for Feedback

As much as feedback and reviews are important for App developers, it can be extremely annoying when you are interrupted by a popup asking for you to rate the app or leave feedback. Good news is that there is now a setting to put an end to the constant pestering!

- Open your Settings app
- Tap iTunes & App Store

- Toggle In-App Ratings & Reviews to "Off"

Customize Text Messages When You Ignore a Call

We get it — you're busy and sometimes you have to ignore a call. But rather than leaving your friends and loved ones hanging, the least you can do is send a text. Sometimes you don't have time for that. To help, your iPhone has three pre-written options ("Sorry, I can't talk right now," "I'm on my way," and "Can I call you later?"), and of course the button that lets you type your own text. You may not have known you can customize and overwrite the other three options. Here's how:

- Open your Settings app

- Tap "Phone"
- Tap "Respond with Text"
- Tap which field you want to edit
- Enter new text

Set a Timer Faster

If you rely heavily on your iPhone timer like we do, you should know that there's a faster way to access it!

- Swipe down on your screen to access the Control Center
- Instead of tapping the timer, press and hold it
- Swipe your finger up to increase the time
- Tap "Start"

Create a Custom Memoji

You're probably already familiar with Animoji, but now you can create your own custom animated avatars called Memoji — that looks just like you. Memoji are a silly but personable and fun new way to communicate with your friends and family. Here's how you can create and customize one of your own:

- Open your messages app
- Tap the animoji icon with the monkey on it
- Swipe right to the plus sign and tap New Memoji
- Choose your skin color
- Choose your freckle level
- Choose your hairstyle
- Choose your head shape, age, and chin
- Choose your eye shape, eye color, and eyelashes

- Choose your eyebrows, eyebrow color, and eyebrow shape
- Choose your nose, lip color, and lip shape
- Choose your ears, earrings
- Choose your facial hair and its color
- Choose your eyewear and its color
- Choose your hat and its color

Add Multiple Faces to Face ID

The new iPhone Xs, Xs Max, XR, and the recently discontinued iPhone X all use Face ID to unlock your device. Previously on iOS 11, the tech could only recognize a single face, so anyone else who uses your phone would have to input a passcode to unlock your iPhone. Just as you could register multiple fingerprints with

Touch ID for past iPhones, Apple now lets you register multiple faces to unlock a single device. Here's how to do it!

- Tap Settings
- Tap Face ID & Passcode
- Type in your passcode
- Tap Set Up an Alternate Appearance
- Scan your face and follow the prompts

How To Stop Your Camera from Shooting Video Outside the Frame on the iPhone 11, 11 Pro, or 11 Pro Max

The biggest change this year for iPhones comes with the cameras. All three iPhones get a new ultra-wide camera, which allows the device to capture more of what's in front of you. Not so new this year is the 64 GB base storage, which will fill up fast when shooting in 4K at 60 fps. A new feature will also add to your storage concerns, however, a feature that captures more video than it really should.

You see, Apple puts its new cameras to the test. When shooting video with either the wide camera (all 2019 iPhones) or the telephoto camera (11 Pro and 11 Pro Max only), the next widest camera will also record video by default. That means the wide camera records when shooting in telephoto, or the ultra-wide when shooting in wide. Apple's intention here is to offer you more options in post so you can rotate your video without needing to crop or compromise the integrity of the image.

Sure, it's a helpful feature for those who want it, but there are drawbacks. Maybe you're happy with the way you frame your shots and don't need the extra video from the Ultra Wide camera to fall back on. Maybe you want to save storage on your iPhone. Either way, you can quickly disable this option by heading to Settings -> Camera and disabling the toggle next to "Videos Captured Outside the Frame."

Interestingly, this option isn't enabled by default in photo mode. It's there, but you'll need to manually enable it to make your iPhone to take a photo with the ultra-wide camera when shooting with either the wide or telephoto cameras.

Measure Objects With Your iPhone

It seems like any time you need to measure something, you can never find the tape measure to do it. Now iOS 13 has a built-in measuring tool that you can use to measure rooms and objects. It's not 100% accurate, but it's a useful tool to use when you need to measure an object or the distance between two things in a pinch. See how the app measures up by following these steps:

- Open the Measure App
- Move your iPhone around so the device can analyze the area

- Hold your iPhone so the camera is pointing at the object you want to measure
- Move your iPhone around until you see a white circle with a dot in the middle
- Line the white dot up with the edge of the item you want to measure
- Press the white button with the + sign
- Drag to opposite edge of item
- Press the white button with the + sign
- The app will display the estimated measurement

Limit iPhone Usage With Screen Time

We're absolutely guilty of using our phones too much. If you want to cut back on time spent on social media, online shopping, or scanning headlines, iOS 13 has a new setting called Screen Time that can help. The feature definitely will come in handy for smartphone-addicted kids, too. Here's how to enable Screen Time:

- Tap the Settings App
- Tap Screen Time
- Tap App Limits
- Tap Add Limit
- Tap a Category
- Tap Add
- Select the Time
- Tap the Top Left Arrow to Save

Add Effects to Your Photos

iOS 13 adds some Snapchat-esque photo editing features you can use right within the messaging app. You can add shapes, stickers, some text, or a filter to your selfies or photos immediately after taking them so you can quickly send them to your friends and get back on with your day.

- Open the Messages App
- Tap the Camera icon on the bottom left
- Take a photo or a selfie
- Tap Effects
- Tap Shapes, Text, or Filters
- Drag the objects on your photo
- Press the send button to send the edited image

Make the Most of 3D Touch

To shave off a couple of seconds throughout your day, remember that most iPhones have a setting called 3D Touch. By applying more pressure to the touchscreen, apps can respond by displaying a menu, showing additional content, or playing an animation.

The Camera app, for example, provides a shortcut for taking a selfie, recording video, scanning a QR Code, or taking a portrait photo.

ompare Phones install iOs 13 gm now iPhone 11 news & tips Everything iOS 13 Ultimate iPhone Customization Videography Tips Privacy & Security Social Media Tips health & Fitness series Mobile Movies & TV Tweaks & Hacks Week Gaming iPhone X Tips & Tricks Jailbreaking Cydia Project Fi on iPhone Security Record Calls on iPhone

How To Scan Documents Right to Your iPhone, iCloud, or Third-Party Services with the Files App in iOS 13

As part of the iOS 11 update, Apple added a document scanner function that creates high-quality digital copies of physical documents, but it was only available inside the Notes app. With iOS 13, Apple has built its scanner right into the Files app, enabling you to quickly create PDFs with your iPhone and do more with them.

By including the scanner in Files, scans can be saved locally on the iPhone, on iCloud Drive, or in any third-party app with Files support such as Box, Dropbox, and Google Drive. The scanner supports some powerful features, including scanning documents with portrait and landscape pages, as well as options to scan in color, grayscale, or black and white. It will also compensate for scanning at an angle, skewing the document so that the final image looks like it was scanned head-on.

Many of you may find that you can get rid of third-party scanner apps entirely.

Step 1- Choose Where to Save the Scan

Open the Files app and navigate to where you would like to save the scan. Locations include anywhere in iCloud Drive; third-party cloud storage apps such as Adobe Creative Cloud, Amazon Drive, Baidu Network Disk, Box, Boxcryptor, Dropbox, Google Drive, Microsoft

OneDrive, and SugarSync; and the "On My iPhone" built-in storage to keep the file locally.

If the service you would like to save to doesn't show up, tap the ellipsis (•••) in the upper right of the "Browse" page, then tap "Edit" on the action sheet. From here, you can choose which services you can see in the Files app, but only ones that are currently installed on your device.

If you toggle one on, make sure to open it up from the "Browse" page after hitting "Done" because you may need to authenticate it first with your user credentials before you can read and write from Files. Also, note that apps that use iCloud may show up here too, such as Adobe Scan and Documents by Readdle, but likely will not be able to scan files to them since they are read-only.

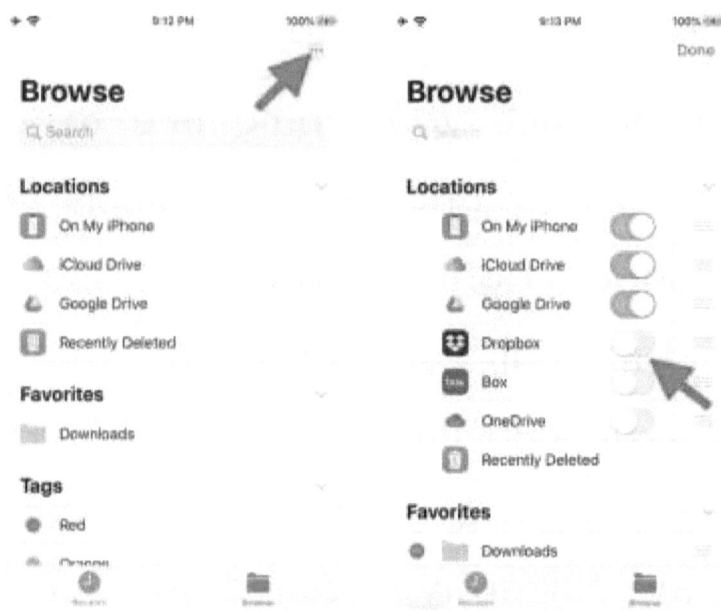

Step 2 - Open the Document Scanner

When you get to where you'd like to save the file, scroll up a bit to expose a hidden toolbar under the search field. Tap the ellipsis (•••) icon, and then tap "Scan Documents."

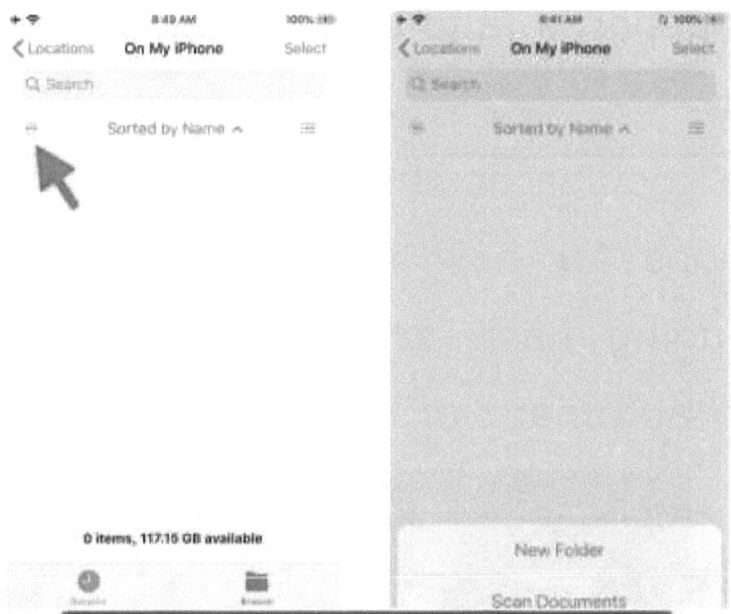

Step 3 - Select Your Scan Options

Placing the document on a surface with good contrast and lighting will help the scanner to find the edges of the paper. For example, a white document on a black table will be easier to scan compared to one placed on a white table.

The scanner can also handle both portrait and landscape documents. Just flip your iPhone sideways to whichever orientation the paper is, and iOS will take care of the rest.

The toolbar at the top gives you a few options for how to scan the document, including flash activation, color options, and automatic or manual scanning.

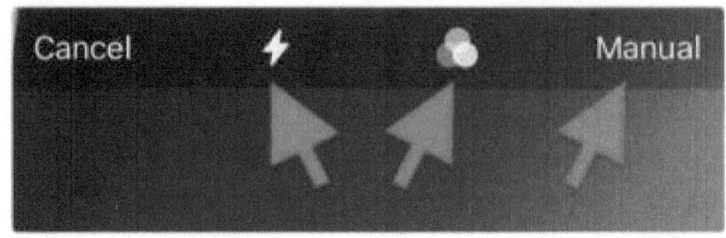

Flash Activation

Tap the lightning bolt icon to view flash options, which include Auto, On, or Off. Generally iOS does an excellent job of knowing when to use the flash, so "Auto" should be fine for most scans. If not, use "On" or "Off" to control the flash manually. If you follow the above suggestions for document placement,

"Auto" or "Off" will give you the best result.

Note: You will likely see a blue box rather than yellow, but it works the same no matter the color.

From the three-circled icon, the color options include Color, Grayscale, Black & White, and Photo. "Color" is best for color documents, while "Grayscale" is best for documents with images that aren't in color. "Black & White" works best for documents that are mostly text and will help create a scan with good contrast. Finally, "Photo" will keep the scans as image files, rather than converting them to a PDF.

If file size is a concern, the "Black & White" option will create the smallest size PDF, followed by "Grayscale," then "Color." The "Photo" option will create the largest files of all of the options.

Shooting Mode

The shooting mode options include Auto or Manual. In "Manual," a blue or yellow box will appear around the document, and it won't scan until you press the shutter button. After that, you'll have the chance to fine-tune where the corners of the paper are, then complete the scan by tapping "Keep Scan" or go back to the scanning screen by tapping "Retake."

With "Auto," iOS will attempt to find the document and automatically scan it. You'll know when it finds the document when you see a blue or yellow box around it, followed by a small spinner and a thumbnail of the image going down to the corner. You can also force iOS to scan early by hitting the shutter button, at which point you can tweak the corners similar to using Manual mode.

Step 4 - Scan the Document

After selecting the scanning options, point the camera at your document. Move the camera around until you see a blue or yellow box surround the document. Hold the camera steady, and iOS will scan the document if using Auto mode. Otherwise, tap the shutter button.

After scanning, you can keep scanning more documents. The "Save" button in the lower right will show how many pages have been scanned, which will later be saved as either a multipage PDF or multiple images. You can also combine portrait and landscape pages in the same set of scans, and the final PDF will accurately reflect their orientation.

If your scans look good, you can tap "Save" to finish up and jump to Step 6. But if you want to make some changes to the color, crop, or orientation, move on to Step 5 below.

Step 5 - Edit the Scan (If Necessary)

Tapping the thumbnail of your scans in the lower left will open the scan editor. Here, you can swipe between all of the scans you've made and edit each of them. You can tweak the edges of the document by tapping the Crop tool in the toolbar, change the Color mode (Color, Grayscale, Black & White, or Photo), or Rotate counterclockwise.

If any pages look particularly bad, you can tap "Retake" to rescan just that page, which will replace it while keeping the pages in the same order they were originally scanned in. Alternatively, you can tap the trash can icon to delete any page completely. When done making edits, tap "Done" to exit the editor.

Step 6 - Save Your Scan

When you've scanned and edited all of your pages, tap the "Save" button in the lower right. A new file in your selected folder will be created named "Scanned Document." Tap the file name, and you can change it to something else. Tap "Done" one more time to save the new name.

However, if you're trying to save a scan or set of scans to a read-only destination, you will have to select another location before you can save. On the modal window, select from any available location. If you choose another read-only one, you'll be prompted to "Choose a new location to save this item." Some cloud storage services will have folders you can't save to, though, you may be able to save to a folder within the prohibited one.

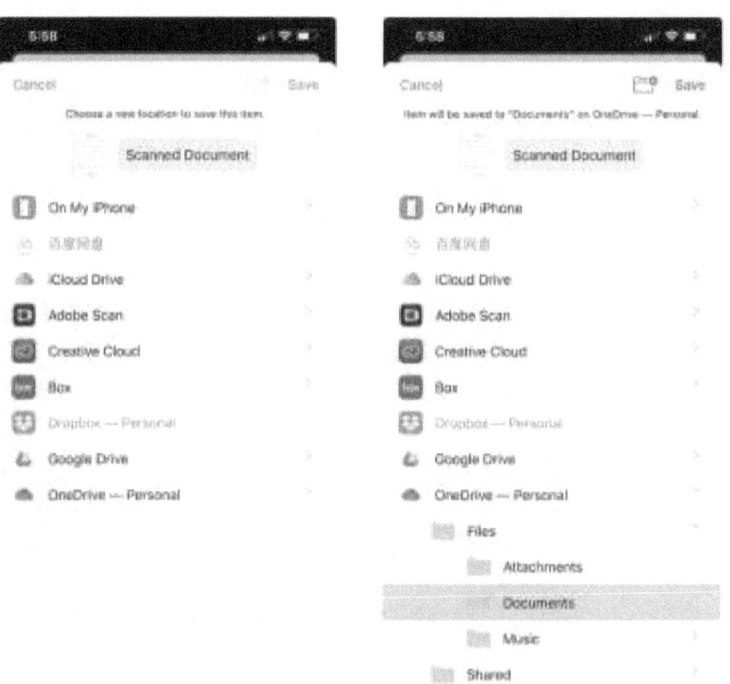

Once you have your file saved, you can treat it like anything else in the Files app. Tap the file to preview it, and tap the Share button to send it to other apps. If it's saved as a PDF, you can also tap the marker icon to use the built-in PDF markup tool to add drawings, text, and shapes. All of this can be done in one place in iOS 13, getting rid of the need to scan a document in Notes only to send it to the Files app to really make use of it.

Create Shortcuts

Besides performance and battery improvements, Shortcuts are probably the most exciting new feature to come from iOS 13. They help simplify everyday tasks and let you get things done with your apps or through Siri. For example, you could create a shortcut called "omw" (on my way) which would open your favorite navigation app, pull up directions to your house, and automatically text your significant other with your estimated travel time. Sounds cool, right? Here's how to create or download shortcuts of your own:

- Open the App Store

- Search Shortcuts

- Download the App

- Open the App

- Tap Get Started

- Tap Gallery at the bottom right

- Tap what shortcut you want to use

- Tap Get Shortcut

- Follow the steps to configure your new shortcut

How To Rotate Photos Without Any Cropping on the iPhone 11, 11 Pro, or 11 Pro Max When Editing

So, you snapped a great picture, but it's just a little off-center. Usually, rotating a photo requires cropping it, which will lower the overall quality of the image. That's not the case on the iPhone 11, 11 Pro, and 11 Pro Max, however. Apple's new flagships allow you to rotate images without cropping them. The only issue? The feature isn't enabled by default.

Before we dive into enabling this option, let's talk about what's really going on here. The iPhone 11, 11 Pro, and 11 Pro Max each come equipped with more than one camera. The iPhone 11 has both a wide camera (1x zoom) and the new ultra-wide camera (0.5x), while the Pros come with the new ultra-wide camera, a wide camera, and a telephoto camera (2x).

So, what does this new feature do with this array of cameras? When you take a photo with either the wide camera or the telephoto camera, the phone will also grab information from the next widest camera.

That means, when shooting with the wide camera, your iPhone will also shoot with the ultra-wide. When shooting with the telephoto camera, your iPhone will also shoot with the wide.

Luckily, enabling the option is as easy as flicking a switch. Just open Settings, choose "Camera," then tap the toggle next to "Photos Captured Outside the Frame." Now, the next time you take a photo with either the wide camera or the telephoto camera, know your next widest camera is also hard at work.

You'll see the fruits of its labor when you use the rotate tool in the new Photos app. Tap "Edit," then tap the cropping tool. Finally, move the slider along the bottom of the display. Instead of cropping your image to fit the new dimensions, your iPhone will simply take the extra data to fill in the gaps.

More of a videographer? You might be interested to hear this feature is also available for video on 2019 iPhones. Unlike in photo mode, however, this feature is enabled by default in video mode. That means less hassle to use the feature, but more of a stress on storage out of the box.

One-Handed Keyboard

Smartphone displays keep getting bigger, which makes typing difficult, especially with one hand. Your iPhone actually has a feature that shifts the keyboard over a smidgen so you can use one hand to type and the other to do whatever else it is that you need to do. Here's how to enable the feature:

- Hold down the emoji or globe icon on the bottom left of the keyboard
- Select the left- or right-handed keyboard icon
- Tap the arrow in the blank space that's created by the keyboard shift to go back to normal

Mute Text-Message Threads

If your friend is the type to send you several short texts rather than one long one, you'll love this tip. It hides text-message alerts so you won't get bombarded with notifications every time you get texts from a specific person or group. It's especially helpful for silencing pesky brands that send you promotions and coupons.

- Open the Messages app
- Swipe left on the text conversation you want to silence
- Tap the Hide Alerts button

Type to Siri

Talking to Siri in public just seems weird. Luckily, you can ask Siri questions with your thumbs instead of your voice. Here's how:

- Tap Settings
- Tap General
- Tap Accessibility
- Tap Siri
- Toggle Type to Siri

Also make sure your phone is on silent, or Siri will blurt out your answer out loud.

Use the Document Scanner in the Notes App

Apple has implemented a convenient document scanner right in the Notes app. Here's how you access it:

- Open the Notes app
- Create a new note or open an existing one

- Tap the + icon that's located above your iPhone's keyboard in the center
- Tap Scan Documents
- Use the shutter button or one of your iPhone's volume buttons to capture a photo of your document
- Adjust the corners of the document by tapping and dragging them, if necessary
- Tap Save

Edit Screenshots

Did you know your iPhone lets you edit your screenshots before saving or sharing them? Here's how to get it:

- Take a screenshot by pressing the power button and the home button at the same time

- Quickly tap the thumbnail of the screenshot that appears at the bottom left of your screen
- From there you can crop the screenshot, doodle on it, highlight parts, etc.
- When you're finished editing, tap Done in the top left, or tap the share icon in the top right to send it to someone

Check Flight Status

If you have to pick someone up from the airport, you'll dig this. Safari makes it much easier to track flights, so you know what time your friend will land and if their flight experiences any delays. If you're the one flying, it comes in handy for figuring out what gate you need to go to and informing you of the total duration of your flight (that way you know how many episodes of Twin Peaks you need to download, of course). Here's how to do it:

- Open Safari
- In the address bar, type the airline's name and the flight number
- Under the Flight tab, select the flight by tapping it
- From there you can see a map of where the flight is and check out the latest information on the flight

How To Connect Your PS4 Controller to Your iPhone for Easier Gameplay

Smartphone hardware surpassed the most popular portable game devices long ago in all but one category — control. Your iPhone is more than capable of running impressive, fully-realized games, but touch controls only go so far. That's why it's so exciting that Apple has added support for PS4 and Xbox controllers with iOS 13.

External controller support isn't necessarily new to iOS. Before iOS 13, you could buy controllers designed to work with MFi-compatible iPhone games. However, it's tough to stack up to the quality a DualShock 4 Wireless Controller brings to the table. Better yet, any MFi-compatible game will work with PlayStation 4 controllers in iOS 13, so no need to bounce between controllers on a game-by-game basis.

Step 1 - Install iOS 13 (If Not Already Done)

Before all else, if your iPhone isn't running iOS 13, you won't be able to pair your PS4 controller for MFi-compatible games. Only Apple's latest iPhone OS supports PS4 controllers for this type of gameplay, so you'll need to make to update your iPhone before continuing with the steps below.

Step 2 - Enter Pairing Mode on Your PS4 Controller

First, if you're not updated to iOS 13 yet, do so. Unlike Bluetooth 5.0 devices such as AirPods or certain Beats, you can't merely locate your PS4 controller in your iPhone's Bluetooth settings and pair it. Instead, you need to tell your controller to enter pairing mode, which will allow iOS to discover it.

To enter pairing mode, hold down the PlayStation button and the Share button until you see the light bar start repeatedly flashing. That flashing indicates the controller is now in pairing mode, ready to connect to any compatible devices via Bluetooth.

Step 3 - Connect to the Controller in Settings

With your PS4 controller's light bar flashing away, open up "Bluetooth" in the Settings app. (Tip: You can get there from the Control Center now.)

Allow iOS to search for a moment. Then you should see your controller appear at the bottom of the display. Tap on your controller, and iOS should pair with it in seconds. You'll know the controller is paired when iOS says "Connected" and the light bar on your controller shines with one solid color again.

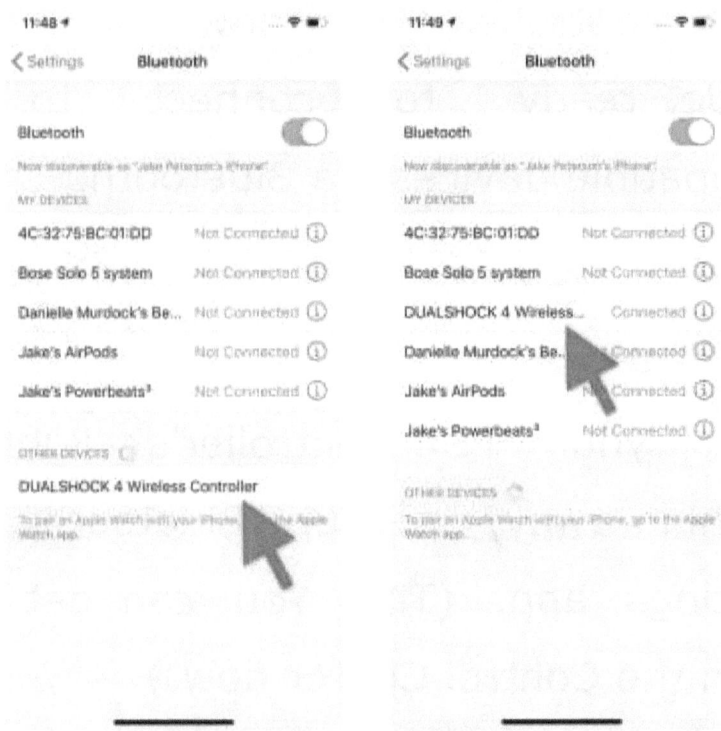

Step 4 - Boot Up a Compatible Game

All that's left to do is to start playing a compatible game. There's no need to pair within the game — if it supports MFi controllers, your PS4 controller will work right away. It's pretty great starting up, say, GTA Vice City, and immediately controlling the game with your DualShock 4 Wireless Controller.

Note: While all MFi-compatible games will work with your PS4 gamepad, you might run into some hiccups while iOS 13 is in beta. If a developer hasn't optimized their games for iOS 13 yet, you might find your PS4 controller won't work.

Step 5 - Disconnect the Controller

While a PS4 controller will power down automatically after a period of inactivity, you'll drain valuable battery life waiting for the controller to do so. If you know you're done playing and simply want to turn off the controller then and there, there are three things you can do. First, press-and-hold the PlayStation button on the control until it turns off, effectively disconnecting from the iPhone in the process.

Your second option: Open the Control Center, long-press on the card in the top left that shows Airplane Mode, Cellular Data, Wi-Fi, and Bluetooth. Then, long-press the Bluetooth icon. After that, tap on "DualShock 4 Wireless Controller" from the list, and it will disconnect automatically.

If it doesn't, you can always fall back on the third option: Head to the "Bluetooth" settings page again, the long way or the Control Center way. Locate your controller from "My Devices," then tap the (i) icon next to its name. On the following page, tap "Disconnect," which will promptly turn off the controller.

The best part? You don't need to return to this page to connect the controller again. As long as you don't connect the controller to another device, press the PlayStation button like normal, and the controller will pair to your iPhone automatically. If it doesn't, just bring up the Control Center and access the

Bluetooth list, then tap on the controller to connect it.

Offload Unused Apps

You've probably gotten a "Storage Almost Full" message a handful of times, and you may have even deleted some apps and photos to make room to install iOS 13, especially if you have a 16 GB iPhone. This new feature will save you a ton of stress and space over time. It automatically deletes apps that you don't use without deleting their documents and data. Here's how to offload apps and save precious storage space:

- Tap Settings
- Tap iTunes & App Store
- Toggle Offload Unused Apps at the bottom

- The deleted apps will be grayed-out on your home screen, and they can be reinstalled with a simple tap

Customize Control Center

You may not have known that your Control Center settings are completely customizable. If you want, you can place the settings and features you use most right where you want them. Here's how:

- Tap Settings
- Tap Control Center
- Tap Customize Controls
- Tap the green "+" icon next to any item you want to add and the red "-" icon to delete items
- Tap, hold, and slide the icon with three bars to reorganize the controls

- Once you're done, tap Back at the top left of your screen

- Swipe up from the bottom of your screen to access Control Center and get a feel for its new, customized layout

Do Not Disturb While Driving

Apple hopes to prevent accidents and cut down on distractions while driving with this new feature. It blocks incoming calls, texts, and notifications when your iPhone detects acceleration or connects to your vehicle's Bluetooth. When someone tries to get a hold of you, your iPhone will send an auto-reply message to let the person know you're driving. The feature can be disabled for passengers, and if there's an emergency and someone needs to reach you, they can still contact you if they respond to the text message with the word "urgent." To turn on the settings, just do the following:

- Tap Settings
- Tap Do Not Disturb
- Tap Automatically if you want the setting to be enabled when detecting movement
- Tap While Connected to Car Bluetooth if your car has Bluetooth
- Tap Manually if you don't want the setting to enable automatically, and then add Do Not Disturb While Driving to Control Center (see previous tip above)
- Tap Auto-Reply to customize and change the message, if you wish

- Tap Auto-Reply To if you want to change who gets sent the auto-reply message. You can pick All Contacts, Favorites, Recent Contacts, or No-One

How You Can Turn Your Live Photos into Videos in iOS 13

Live Photos are a fun way to relive memories, but there's a problem: unless you're only friends with Apple users, sharing Live Photos isn't quite as fun. Without a third-party converter, you can't share your Live Photo in all its moving glory. That is, until iOS 13, where you can quickly turn your Live Photos into videos.

Converting a Live Photo in iOS 13 is super easy. Simply open Photos, then open the Live Photo in question. Next, tap the share button in the bottom-right corner of the display, then scroll down and tap "Save as Video." If your Live Photo is stored in iCloud Photo Library, it'll need to download first. You'll then see iOS saving the new video.

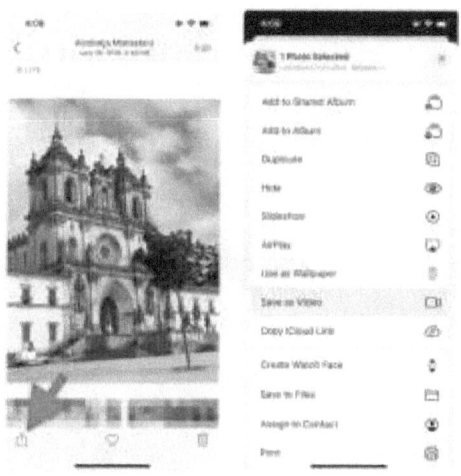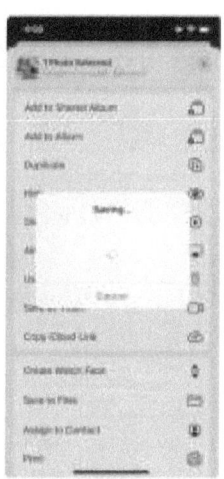

Once complete, you can head to your Videos folder or "All Photos" to share the once Live Photo to your heart's content. Just keep in mind this video will have the same time and date as your Live

Photo, so it will be sorted accordingly in your library.

If you don't see this option here, it's likely you have a Live Photo effect enabled. Swipe up on the Live Photo to reveal the effects browser. If either "Loop," "Bounce," or "Long Exposure" are enabled, simply tap "Live," and repeat the steps above.

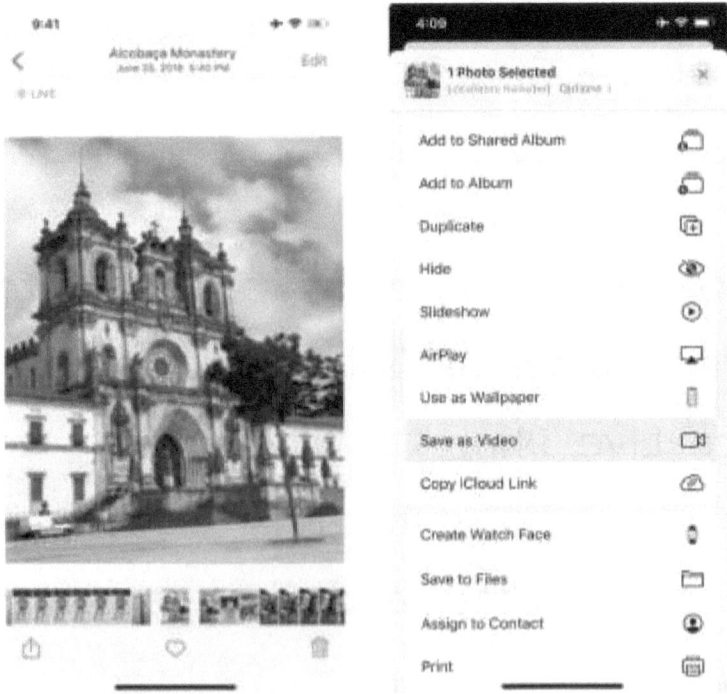

Text Replacement

Sometimes typing things like email addresses, URLs, and, of course, shruggy ¯_(ツ)_/¯ is a pain. Your iPhone has a text-replacement feature that lets you type just a few characters rather than spending forever typing the actual thing. Here's how you do it:

- Open the Settings app
- Tap General
- Tap on Keyboard
- Tap on Text Replacement
- Tap the + on the top right corner
- In the Phrase field, type the word or phrase you want to create a shortcut for

- In the Shortcut field, type the text you want to be replaced by the phrase

- Tap Save at the top right corner

Now, any time you type the shortcut on your keyboard, your iPhone will replace it with the phrase after you press the space bar.

Hey Siri

We have a love-hate relationship with Siri. Siri may not be as smart as Alexa on our Amazon Echo, but Siri is much more portable. To make Siri even more accessible, you should enable Hey Siri, which lets you use Siri without pressing the home button on your iPhone. Here's how you turn it on:

- Open the Settings app

- Scroll down and select Siri

- Toggle to Allow "Hey Siri!"

Tip: If you ever lose your iPhone at home, just shout "Hey Siri" and you should hear a tone. Keep doing it until you find your phone. Sure, you can always log into iCloud and use Find My iPhone, but this method is just as effective, and it takes less time.

Teach Siri How to Correctly Pronounce Names

Siri may not be saying your friend's name correctly, but you can fix that!

- Hold the home button or say, "Hey, Siri" to trigger Siri

- Say, "That's not how you pronounce [name.]"

- Say your friend's name

- Siri will offer four pronunciation options
- Select the correct pronunciation

Custom Vibrations

You may already have custom ringtones for when certain friends and loved ones call, but that doesn't come in handy when you have your phone on silent though. Your iPhone lets you create and assign custom vibrations to specific contacts. Here's what you have to do:

- Open the Settings app
- Select Sounds & Haptics
- Select Ringtone
- Select Vibration
- Tap Create New Vibration
- Create a new vibration by tapping and holding however you want

- Tap Stop in the bottom right
- Tap Save in the top right
- Name the vibration

After you create the custom vibration, here's what you need to do to assign it to a contact:

- Open the Contacts app
- Choose the contact you want to assign the custom vibration to do.
- Tap Edit on the top right corner
- Select Vibration
- Choose the new vibration that you created earlier

Use your Keyboard as a Trackpad

You may not have known that your iPhone's keyboard can double as a trackpad. This way you can move your cursor much more accurately instead of tapping and holding on the screen to bring up the magnifying glass. To use this feature, you need an iPhone 6S or later.

- While you are typing a message, firmly press and hold anywhere on the keyboard to activate the trackpad
- Drag your finger around to move your cursor through the text
- When the cursor is where you want it to be, just let go

If you have an older iPhone that doesn't have 3D touch, we recommend you install the third-party keyboard, Gboard, which lets you use the spacebar as a mini trackpad to swipe through text.

Tip:

Rather than tapping the 123 button at the bottom left of the keyboard, tapping the character you want, and then tapping the 123 button again, just hold the 123 button, slide your thumb to the character you want to use, then lift your thumb up off your screen. The character will be input, and your keyboard will return to normal without taking the extra step of tapping the 123 button again.

Use Your iPhone as a Level

Most people rarely use the Compass app that's preinstalled on their iPhone. Within the app is another tool you may not have known about: a spirit level. Here's how you easily access it:

- Open up the Measure app
- Tap Level at the bottom right

- Lay your phone flat against the surface you need to check levelness for

If you tap the screen, you can measure the difference between the two surfaces. The red margin shows how much the two angles vary.

Turn on Medical ID Section

Within Apple's Health app, you should fill out the Medical ID section. This will not only come in handy in the event of an actual emergency, but it can also help a good Samaritan return your iPhone if you lose it.

- Open the Health app
- Tap Medical ID at the bottom right
- Tap Edit at the top right

- Make sure Show When Locked is toggled

- Fill out the corresponding text boxes, and put your email or social media handles in the medical notes section so someone can return your lost phone

Hide Photos

Sometimes you have photos in your camera roll that your mom wouldn't be proud of. When you hand your iPhone over to someone else, they may swipe and see something you wouldn't want them to. Fortunately, you can prevent that from happening by hiding certain photos.

- Open the photos app

- Open the album where the photo(s) you want to hide reside

- Tap Select at the top right

- Select the photo(s) you want to hide

- Tap the share icon at the bottom left

- Tap the hide icon at the bottom right

- Tap Hide Photo

Set a Sleep Timer

If you like to listen to music or podcasts before you fall asleep, you're going to love this trick. The iPhone includes a timer in the clock app that can stop audio playback from any app.

- Open the Clock app

- Select Timer at the bottom right

- Set how long you want the timer to be
- Tap When Timer Ends
- Scroll to the bottom of the list and tap Stop Playing
- Tap Set at the top right of your screen
- Press the Start button
- Drift off to sleep without worrying about your iPhone battery being dead in the morning from leaving your music on.

Disable Swipe Typing in Apple's iOS 13 Keyboard

One core theme with each new iteration of iOS is the introduction of at least one or two features that fans have been hoping to see for years. With iOS 13, that feature is swipe typing, a first for the native iOS keyboard. While some of us have been getting our glide-typing fix with apps like Gboard for years, you might find swiping isn't quite your style. Luckily, the feature is easy to disable.

Swipe typing, or "Slide to Type" as Apple calls it, is far from the only new and exciting addition to iOS in 2019. System-wide dark mode, a redesigned Reminders app, and "Look Around" in Maps are just a few of the more than 200 new features you'll find in iOS 13. If you're not a fan of Slide to Type, you'll likely find yourself enjoying plenty of other changes the latest iPhone update has to offer.

Disabling Slide to Type is as simple as a few taps. First, head to Settings ->

General -> Keyboards. Alternatively, you can launch this settings page from the keyboard itself by long-pressing the keyboard switcher, then by tapping "Keyboard Settings." That switcher will appear as either the Emoji icon or the Globe icon, depending on your keyboard setup. Note, if you only have one keyboard enabled, neither icon will appear so use the Settings app.

193

Once in "Keyboards," simply locate "Slide to Type" from the options list and tap the toggle to disable the feature. That's it. Now, you'll find sliding around the keyboard does exactly what it did before — nothing. If you ever want Slide to Type back, re enable the toggle. Just be aware that swiping curse words is a hassle since Apple made profanity a pain in the ass.

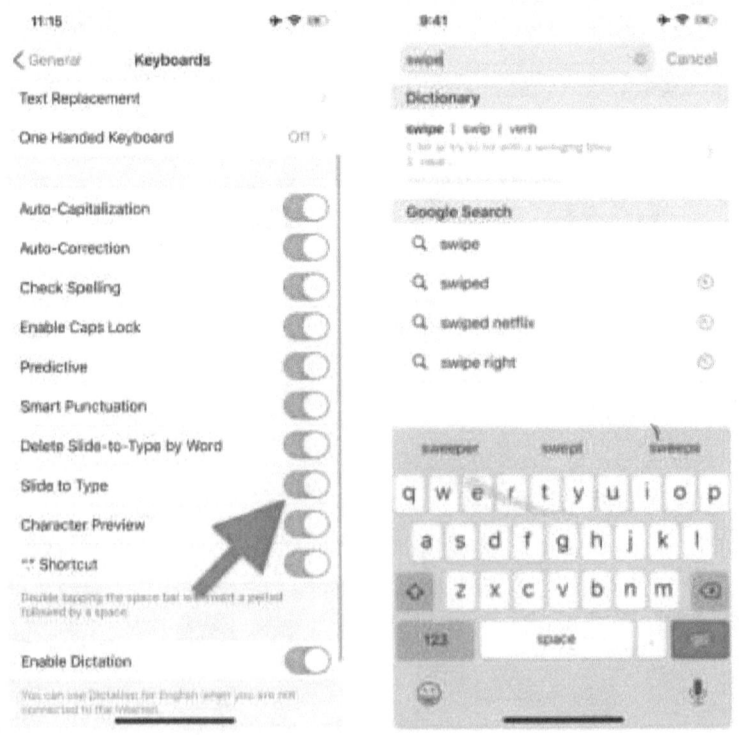

How to Place the Cursor, Make Selections, Perform Edits & More

Navigating and editing text is an essential part of any operating system, and with iOS 13, Apple has made some significant changes. Some things remain the same when working with text, but there are many updates to moving the cursor, scrolling, and selecting, cutting, copying, pasting, undoing, and redoing text.

Apple streamlined the text editing system to make it easier and quicker to use on an iPhone. So the changes to editing text in iOS 13 go relatively deep. Apple even ditched the magnifying glass that'd appear when moving the cursor, something that has been around since the very first iPhone.

Text selection is also faster, allowing you to highlight text with either a swipe or a few taps, in addition to the drag handles that previous versions of iOS relied on. Also, while not explicitly geared toward text, the scroll bar is now draggable. So you can quickly move to any point in a document in one step instead of having to swipe over and over.

While some of the things below also apply to selectable, non-editable text, there will be some differences. We're just focusing on the editing side of things.

Before iOS 13, moving the cursor could be done in a few different ways. All of the following ways worked in iOS 12, and some of them still work in iOS 13 (which will be noted).

- **Tap**: The cursor can be moved to the beginning or end of a word, number, emoticon, emoji, and so on, depending on where you tap on the word. It allows you to jump around a text field quickly, and it's sticking around in iOS 13, though, with a minor change as you'll see.

- **Tap-and-hold**: In editable text, the tap-and-hold action brings up a magnified view of what's under your finger to allow you to place the cursor where you want it precisely. Though precise, it's a bit slow, requiring a tap-and-hold every time you want to drag the cursor somewhere else. It's been around since the first iPhone, but it's not found in iOS 13.

- **Press-and-slide on the keyboard:** Introduced in iOS 9 with the addition of 3D Touch, a firm press on the keyboard turns it into a trackpad that can be used to move the cursor around. On iPhones without 3D Touch, iOS 12 added long-pressing the space bar to the same effect. Additionally, iPads can access the trackpad by using either the long-press on the space bar or by dragging with two fingers. All of these methods are still available in iOS 13.

- **External keyboards**: If using a hardware keyboard, the cursor can be moved by using the arrow keys. And there are different ways to move the cursor by using the arrow keys in combination with the modifier keys. All of that works as expected in iOS 13.

The most significant change to cursor movement comes with the removal of the tap-and-hold method to bring up the magnifying glass. In iOS 13, the cursor becomes draggable. Now, rather than tapping, holding, and waiting for the magnifying glass to show up, you can just grab the cursor and move it right where you want it. After grabbing the cursor, it will hover right above your finger, so you can still see and drop it precisely where you want to.

It's easily the most disruptive change in iOS 13 and will require some users to change a habit that's been built up for the past decade. Once your muscle memory switches to the new system, however, moving around the text cursor should become quicker since there's no waiting on the magnifying glass.

The tap method also received a small tweak in iOS 13. In prior versions, after tapping a word to move the cursor, a second tap will only open the edit menu. Plus, if you tap to put the cursor inside of a word after the first tap, it would only move the cursor to the beginning or end, not in the middle anywhere.

In iOS 13, if you tap to go to a word, then tap in the same spot, the edit menu will appear. But if you tap that word the second time in the middle somewhere, the cursor will move to the place within the word that you touched, as well as open the edit menu.

Selecting & Moving Text

Prior to iOS 13, selecting text could be done in a few different ways. Some of those ways continue to work in Apple's latest operating system for the iPhone.

- **Double-tap**: Tap twice on a word, number, etc. to select it and open up the contextual edit menu with options to Cut, Copy, Paste, BIU, Look Up, Speak, Share, Indent Right/Left, and Spell. You can drag the ends to expand the selection. The gesture still works in iOS 13 but there are also similar options that do more (see below).

- **Long-press a word**: If you long-press (but not too hard) the word, number, etc., it will be highlighted and the contextual edit menu appears. In it, you can Cut, Copy, Paste, BIU, Look Up, Speak, Share, Indent Right/Left, and Spell. You can drag the ends to expand the selection. On non-3D Touch devices, long-pressing brings up the cursor magnifier instead. It's all there in iOS 13 except for the cursor magnifier, and you may see some small changes in the edit menu.

- **Long-press a word and slide**: On 3D Touch devices, when you long-press a set of characters to highlight it, without releasing your finger from the screen, you can drag to select more text. All of the edit menu options for the long-press show up except Speak. In iOS 13, it works the same, though, you have to wait for haptic feedback.

- **Tap the cursor:** When you tap the cursor in its place, the contextual edit menu appears with options to Select, Select All, Paste, Insert Drawing, BIU, Indent Right/Left, and Speak Sentence. You can drag the ends to expand the selection. All of it works in iOS 13.

- **Move the cursor:** Just like with tapping the cursor itself, after moving the cursor with the tap-and-hold action, you'll see all the same options. While tap-and-hold doesn't work in iOS 13 for moving the cursor, dragging the cursor has the same effect.

- **Hard-press a word**: On 3D Touch devices, when you hard-press a word, number, etc., it jumps into a floating bubble that you can place anywhere else in the text. It's basically a shortcut for moving a single set of characters. Unfortunately, it no longer works in iOS 13.

- **External keyboards:** Holding down the Shift key and using the arrow keys and modifiers to move the cursor will highlight the text and show the contextual edit menu where appropriate.

In iOS 13, the double-tap method has been updated to include triple and quadruple taps. So you can do more with multiple taps than just select a word. Tapping to highlight now includes the following options:

- Tap twice to highlight a single word.
- Tap three times to highlight a single sentence.
- Tap four times to highlight an entire paragraph.

As mentioned above, the "long-press a word and slide" action works similarly, but you must wait for haptic feedback to know that it's ready to select more text. If you select a word without getting the haptic feedback, you'll just drag the whole selector box over to another word or set of characters.

Additionally, the "Indent Right" and "Indent Left" edit menu options are now labeled as "Indentation." When you tap that, you get options to "Increase" and "Decrease" the indent.

Also worth mentioning, whenever you tap on a word, then tap in the middle of it somewhere, the cursor will jump there, and the edit menu will appear with options to Select, Select All, Paste, Insert Drawing, BIU, and Indentation.

Editing Text

In previous versions of iOS, getting to the Cut, Copy, and Paste commands is primarily done using the contextual edit menu that appears when text or numbers are selected, as seen above. It's not the fastest way, but it's better than the options for Undo and Redo. Introduced almost a decade ago, the "Shake to Undo" and "Redo" feature may be responsible for its fair share of broken iPhone screens.

To get around those downfalls, some apps added buttons to their UI for oft-used features, and Apple even added them to the top of the onscreen keyboard on the iPad. However, both have shortcomings in that they aren't available across iOS and are usually only shown when editing text.

In iOS 13, Apple has added some new three-finger gestures to make accessing these commands much faster across all of the system. Much like keyboard shortcuts, learning these gestures will make manipulating text much quicker and fluid. To get started, select some text, then do the following:

- Pinch with three fingers to copy.
- Pinch with three fingers twice in succession to cut.
- Do a three-finger spread to paste.
- Swipe to the left with three fingers to undo.
- Swipe to the right with three fingers to redo.

- Tap with three fingers to open the menu.

When you perform each gesture, a small bubble will appear at the top of the screen showing which command was executed. These gestures tend to work better on larger iPhone models. If you're on an iPhone with a smaller screen (the iPhone SE, in particular), you can also do a three-finger tap to open a menu at the top of the screen with all five commands available. But you can also use that option if the swipe gestures are too hard to remember.

Scrolling Through Documents

The iPhone has always done a great job providing a fast and smooth scrolling experience. Flicking a webpage then watching it scroll and slowly come to a stop was one of those "wow" moments back when the iPhone first came out. The experience has aged well for the most part, but it can be a little frustrating when scrolling through long documents.

For iOS 12 and under, you can get back to the top by tapping the status bar, but getting to a specific point is often an exercise in frustration. Usually, you would start to flick over and over, only to scroll past where you wanted to go since things are moving so fast.

In iOS 13, Apple has finally added the ability to grab and move the scroll bar. To do it, scroll a bit to show the scroll bar on the right side of the screen, then long press on it. You'll feel a haptic tap and the scroll bar will get thicker. Now, just move it up and down the side of the screen to scroll to any point. No more flicking!

Working with editable text documents in iOS 13 is going to take some getting used to for people who have been using iOS for several years. While many of the old ways of doing things are sticking around, functions like moving the cursor are changing concepts that have been there since the iPhone was first unveiled.

Ultimately, learning the new methods to work with text can make using iOS faster and more fluid, and it can possibly save you from an expensive "Shake to Undo" screen repair.

Thank you for purchasing our manual and we believed you have learned a lot of tips and tricks that has helped you master your new iPhone 11 series and iOS 13.

www.ingramcontent.com/pod-product-compliance
Lightning Source LLC
Chambersburg PA
CBHW030620220526
45463CB00004B/1361